A Core Collection In Dance

Mary E. Edsall
Editor

Editorial Committee

Nancy E. Friedland
Monica Moseley
Patricia Rader

Compiled by

Dance Librarians Committee
Association of College and Research Libraries

Association of College and Research Libraries
A division of the American Library Association
Chicago, 2001

The paper used in this publication meets the minimum requirements of
American National Standard for Information Sciences–Permanence of Paper
for Printed Library Materials, ANSI Z39.48—1992.∞

Library of Congress Cataloging-in-Publication Data
A core collection in dance / Mary E. Edsall, editor ; compiled by Dance Librarians
Committee, Association of College and Research Libraries.
    p. cm.
  Includes index.
  ISBN 0-8389-8118-6 (alk. paper)
    1. Dance--Bibliography. I. Edsall, Mary E. II. Association of College and Research
Libraries. Dance Librarians Committee.

Z7514.D2 C685 2001
[GV1594]
016.7928--dc21

                                2001027794

Printed in the United States of America.

05 04 03 02 01   5 4 3 2 1

Table of Contents

ACKNOWLEDGEMENTS

In compiling and editing this book I have been assisted in many ways by a number of individuals and organizations. I especially wish to acknowledge my sincere appreciation to all of the librarians, faculty, and independent scholars and researchers whose names appear in the list of contributors. Grateful appreciation is due the Editorial Committee members, including Nancy E. Friedland, Monica Moseley, and Pat Rader. Thanks also go to Beth Kerr for developing the indexes, and to Eric A. Kidwell for providing a review of the book in accordance with the Arts Section, Publications Committee standards. I wish to acknowledge Madeleine Nichols, Curator of the Jerome Robbins Dance Division of the New York Public Library for the Performing Arts for all of her advice and support by hosting the meetings of the Editorial Committee and providing technical assistance. This publication of this book would not have been possible without the ongoing support of the Dance Librarians Committee of the Arts Section of the Association of College and Research Libraries, American Library Association, and the initial coordination of the work by Mary Strow. For continued support of my research, I wish to thank Maureen Pastine, University Librarian at Temple University and Dr. Luke Kahlich, Chair, Department of Dance at Temple University. Special thanks go to Hugh Thompson, Director of Publications at ACRL for his direction, assistance, and patience for more than five years and for his skill in designing the book. *A Core Collection in Dance* is dedicated to Barbara Palfy and to the memory of Robert Ellis Dunn, who continue to be inspirational to the profession of dance librarianship.

INTRODUCTION
Mary E. Edsall

A Core Collection in Dance, is the result of a collective endeavor within the fields of dance librarianship and dance research. Initially, a project publication of the Dance Librarians Committee of the Arts Section of the American Library Association (ALA), the final product represents a collaborative effort of dance librarians and archivists, as well as dance scholars and researchers. This introduction describes the process of the first effort devoted to identifying the essential published literature in dance, outlines the scope and content, and addresses the implications for future research devoted to finding the essential literature within an emerging body of scholarship representing the ephemeral art of the dance.

In the late 1980s, as a graduate student in dance at Columbia University, I produced a thesis on the topic of collection development in dance specifically focused on identifying what is considered core literature to the field of dance research. In my course of study, I found virtually no adequate printed resources on the subject and very few trained professionals to guide my research. While my thesis represented a very rudimentary effort, my interest had been fueled and my dedication to the development and perpetuation of dance librarianship as a profession had increased. Subsequently, as a student in the MLS degree program at the University of Maryland, I had the opportunity to work in the music library. Under the direction of head reference librarian, Philip Vandermeer, I conducted an analysis of the library's holdings in dance. I weeded and developed the music library's collection in dance, using a study that had been prepared a few years earlier by former NYPL dance librarian, Barbara Palfy. Through the efforts of one of Maryland's dance faculty, Robert Ellis Dunn (former assistant curator at the Dance Collection at the NYPL), Palfy had been solicited to prepare a guide outlining what she considered to be the essential published sources that would support the university's programs and curricula in dance. This document was the only guide to collection development in dance for college and research libraries available at that time and served as a resource in the development of *A Core Collection in Dance*.

However, my investigations and discoveries were certainly not new or unique. It has long been a recognized dilemma in dance research that there exist no adequate resources to assist librarians or faculty in developing and maintaining library collections sufficient in supporting curricula or research in dance at the college and university level. In fact, the National Association of Schools of Dance (NASD), the national organization responsible for the accreditation of dance education facilities, has only a paragraph or two in its guidelines devoted to the qualifications for library and resource centers within schools of dance. Moreover, the existing tools to catalog and index dance, such as the Library of Congress subject headings are not comprehensive and reflect a geographic bias toward western dance forms. To complicate matters, in the past fifteen years the dance field has produced a large and rigorous body of scholarship that is more global in perspective, and more reflective of the multidisciplinary nature of research in dance. The deficits in the science of collecting and cataloging published materials in dance, coupled with the emergence of new dance scholarship, has revealed the major problem facing the field of dance today—there is no common language used to create or define the literature of dance. Indeed, there is no standardized language used to communicate the art itself. This lack of common language, I believe, is a primary contributor to the perception of dance as the most ephemeral form of art.

In 1996, while I was chair of the Dance Librarians Committee of the American Library Association, the committee decided to devote its efforts to compiling and producing a collection development tool for dance. Under the initial coordination of Indiana University librarian, Mary Strow, work towards producing the ACRL publication, *A Core Collection in Dance* began. At the annual meeting of the ALA in New York in 1996, more than twenty-five library professionals with responsibilities for collection development in dance and related areas met in the cafeteria of the New York Public Library to design a strategy for compiling the bibliography. With LCSH being the only system of categorization agreed upon to use as a loose guide, and a somewhat underdeveloped understanding of what a core collection means to dance, we collectively set out to compile the bibliography. Through Strow's coordinating work, subject categories were assigned to individuals, who produced the various sections. The result was overwhelming. What we had created was a voluminous, nonstandardized, nonuniform collection of titles that were bound together more by a need to gather the information as opposed to categorizing the literature by subject and defining it as essential. We had found the research to fit our rather loose methodology, as opposed to finding the methodology appropriate to the research. There was a great variance in the data collected by each individual as a variety of levels of subject expertise and degrees of intellectual strategies for categorization had been employed in collecting the data.

When it came time to conduct the first edit of the monograph, Strow had accepted a visiting librarian position in Australia and effectively placed the responsibility of editing and bringing the work to publication into my hands. I realized I could not do this on my own and needed assistance in converting the bibliography into a work that was legitimate and usable. In the winter of 1998, I formed an editorial committee, which included Nancy Friedland from Columbia University, Pat Rader, head cataloger in the Dance Division of the NYPL, and Monica Moseley, assistant curator in the Dance Division of the NYPL. Together, we worked on renovating the structure, revising the content, and editing the style of the core collection bibliography.

In the process, it became apparent that a vast amount of literature, in some areas representing the dance of entire continents, was lacking. We enlisted the assistance of dance scholars and faculty with expertise in those areas to provide or revise many of the sections. The result evolved into a collaborative effort within the field of dance with contributions from forty subject experts as well as generalists in dance research and dance librarianship. Without this cooperation, the bibliography would not have developed as an effective instrument in providing selective access to the wide body of dance literature.

In conducting the final edit, I discovered certain perspectives in literature of the field had changed, affecting the structure and arrangement of the content of the bibliography. Additionally, through recent scholarly research, I have had the opportunity to access and manipulate more literature within a wide variety of genres. As a result of the observations I have made regarding the scope, content, methodologies, and applications of dance research, I further revised the genre terminology and content of some sections. In addition, I revised the introductions to reflect a more uniform approach and a global perspective in categorization and access.

A Core Collection in Dance represents a comprehensive core selection of the most credible and noteworthy works of existing print and nonprint literature from an emergent field of scholarship. It is appropriate for use by dance librarians, faculty, scholars, and researchers to use in building and evaluating library collections that support broad-based liberal curricula in dance or that support major repositories of dance research resources. However, it can also be used as a point of departure in researching the resources necessary to support more specifically focused programs and collections. Although juvenile literature is not included, materials that are of use to secondary education can be located through a specific selection process. The book may also serve to identify strengths and weaknesses in areas or aspects of the dance literature.

Titles of printed literature, including books, periodical publications (not articles), moving image materials, and new media resources, are included. Primarily, selections are not annotated unless the selection is so ambiguous as to warrant an explanatory note. Dissertations, technical reports, and some forms of gray literature have been included when those titles represent the only significant authoritative work on a core subject. Because the interdisciplinary nature of dance has made the categorization quite challenging, many of the works are cross-referenced in more than one category. However, the majority of titles are individually placed in the section most relevant to the major emphasis of the work. Most of the works have been written in the English language, although important works in other languages have been included.

Each section begins with an introductory statement. A brief overview or statement as to the nature or definition of the genres may be included as well as a statement explaining the consideration that led to the selection and organization of titles within each category. Within each introduction other sections that may contain relevant materials are also listed. Electronic and Internet resources, including listservs and world wide web sites have been included, but only those that have sustained changes in the electronic information industry and remain now as meta-sites and established listservs. Indexes of geographical locations and names, as well as terms and concepts, are included at the end of the volume for ready reference.

Historically, the publication of dance literature has tended not to enjoy large print runs, and volumes are often not reprinted, thus many titles are out of print. Because of this fluid nature of the publication practice of dance works, titles that have gone out of print have not been identified as out of print. However, many out-of-print titles can be obtained through dealers. Lists of out-of-print book dealers and moving image distributors are listed; readers are advised that this information is also time-sensitive and should be checked for accuracy. Also included are the addresses of the publishers of periodicals that are recommended for subscription.

A Core Collection in Dance serves not only as a model for collection development but also as an important development in the field of dance research. Indeed, it is a first attempt at identifying the essential works of an ephemeral art form and defining a classification system for access to those works. Classification systems for providing access to the literature of the dance need to be improved and standardized on a national level and applied within local access systems. However, for dance these standards must first be developed before they can be improved and revised, and those changes must be reflective of the evolving nature of the dance in performance, research, and the resulting documentation. While the LCSH remains an inadequate classification system, it cannot simply be replaced by the use of keyword searching. The root of the problem lies in the lack of commonly used language to communicate the creation of dance phenomena. In addition, there is no standardized language used to document those phenomena in the form of primary resources and published literature. Moreover, a common language is needed to describe and classify the documentation and literature, as well as the data and meta-data used to provide access to the documents of the dance. If access is the goal of dance librarianship, then the vision of dance through the creators of the phenomena, the collectors and authors of the documentation, and the literature of the phenomena must be considered in developing models for collection development and intellectual access. The most important accomplishment of *A Core Collection in Dance*, through its development as a collective endeavor, is that the work in and of itself is indicative of the symbiotic relationship between dance research and dance librarianship—an important relationship that needs to be nurtured and strengthened.

Contributors

Lisa Arkin is an independent dance scholar residing in Oregon.

Kariamu Welsh Asante is professor of dance in the dance department at Temple University.

Virginia L. Brooks is professor of motion pictures and television at Brooklyn College.

Mary Cargill is reference librarian in the humanities division of the Columbia University Libraries.

Nena Couch is curator and associate professor of the Jerome Lawrence and Robert E. Lee Theatre Research Institute of Ohio State University.

Oliver J. Cutshaw is the binding librarian in the Harvard College Library at Harvard University.

Mary E. Edsall is a dance archivist and scholar in Philadelphia, and was Assistant Curator of the Harvard Theatre Collection from 1996-1998.

Martha Eddy is on the faculty of the Program in Dance and Dance Education at Teachers College, Columbia University.

Paula Epstein is coordinator of Library Outreach at Columbia College in Chicago.

Katy Farrell, performer and researcher on Middle Eastern dance, is reference and bibliographic instruction librarian at SUNY Geneseo.

Michelle Forner is a Middle Eastern dance performer and teacher in California, and former director of the Dance Heritage Coalition.

Nancy E. Friedland is assistant undergraduate and media services librarian in the humanities division of the Columbia University Libraries.

Judith Gelernter was the librarian for the Dance Notation Bureau in New York City from 1995–1997, and is presently the library director at the Union Club, New York City.

Jane Gottlieb is associate vice president for library and information resources, The Juilliard School, New York City.

Kim Hale is acquisitions librarian and coordinator of collection development at Columbia College in Chicago.

Constance Valis Hill is on the faculty of the Five Colleges Consortium in Massachusetts.

Judith Brin Ingber is the founding director of Voices of Sepherad, and is on the faculty at the University of Minnesota.

Jonathan David Jackson is a University Presidential Fellow in the Dance Department at Temple University.

Catherine J. Johnson is the founding director of the Dance Heritage Coalition.

Adrienne L. Kaeppler is curator (Oceania), National Museum of Natural History, at the Smithsonian Institution.

Luke Kahlich is chair of the dance department at Temple University.

Beth Kerr is a librarian at the undergraduate library at the University of Texas, Austin.

Eric A. Kidwell is director of Houghton Memorial Library at Huntingdon College in Alabama.

Dorothy Lourdou was chief cataloger at the dance division, The New York Public Library for the Performing Arts from 1968 until her retirement in 2000.

Paula Matthews is associate librarian and music librarian at Bates College.

Joellen A. Meglin is associate professor in the dance department at Temple University.

Morocco, also known as Carolina Varga Dinicu, has researched, performed and taught Middle Eastern dance for over forty years.

Monica Moseley is assistant curator of the dance division, The New York Public Library for the Performing Arts.

Madeleine Nichols is curator of the dance division, The New York Public Library for the Performing Arts.

Karen Nickeson is assistant curator of the Billy Rose Theatre Collection, New York Public Library for the Performing Arts

Charles Perrier is manuscripts librarian at the dance division, The New York Public Library for the Performing Arts.

Michelle Potter is a dance scholar on the staff of Soundscreen Australia in Canberra, Australia.

Patricia Rader is reference librarian and chief cataloger at the dance division, The New York Public Library for the Performing Arts.

Anthony Shay is a retired librarian, and director of AVAZ Dance Theatre.

Susan Spalding is coordinator of the dance program at Berea College in Kentucky.

Alan Stark is librarian for the Biblioteca de las Artes, Centro Nacional de las Artes, Mexico City.

Nancy Stokes is performing and visual arts bibliographer at the University of Akron.

Mary Strow is head of the Health, Physical Education, and Recreation Library, and librarian for dance, theatre, and drama at Indiana University.

Lorelei Tanji is fine arts librarian at University of California, Irvine.

Kim Chandler Vaccaro is on the fine arts/dance faculty of Rider University in New Jersey.

Judy Van Zile is professor in the department of theatre and dance at the University of Hawaii, Honolulu.

General Reference Works

A striking characteristic of reference sources for dance is the overlap with related fields in other disciplines, especially theatre, music and the fine arts. In the past few decades publication of dance literature has increased markedly as dance has begun to achieve recognition as a distinct discipline in its own right. However, much essential and relevant information must still be sought in the general reference sources of related fields. For many years the only truly comprehensive encyclopedia to cover the dance field was the Italian-language *Enciclopedia dello Spettacolo*. The first comprehensive English-language encyclopedia devoted to dance became a reality in 1998 with the publication of the long-awaited *International Encyclopedia of Dance*. A major bibliography of the field, encompassing all forms and types of dance, appeared in 1974 with the publication by the New York Public Library of *The Dictionary-Catalog of the Dance Collection*. This section represents additional core reference sources, including dictionaries, encyclopedias, directories, and indexes.

Dictionaries and Encyclopedias
Print resources

Billman, Larry. *Film Choreographers and Dance Directors: A Heavily-Illustrated Biographical Encyclopedia with A History and Filmographies, 1893–1995*. Jefferson, N.C.: McFarland and Co., 1996.

Blas Vega, Jose, and Manuel Rios Ruiz. *Diccionario Enciclopedico Ilustrado del Flamenco*. 2nd ed. Madrid: Editorial Cinterco, 1990.

Chujoy, Anatole, and P.W. Manchester. *The Dance Encyclopedia*. Rev. ed. New York: Simon and Schuster, 1967. 993 pages.
> An older but still valuable source.

Clarke, Mary, and David Vaughan, eds. *The Encyclopedia of Dance and Ballet*. New York: Putnam, 1977.

Cohen-Stratyner, Barbara. *Biographical Dictionary of the Dance*. Introduction by Lincoln Kirstein. New York: Schirmer, 1982.

Craine, Debra and Judith Mackrell. *The Oxford Dictionary of Dance*. New York: Oxford University Press, 2000.
> This volume supercedes *The Concise Oxford Dictionary of Dance* by Horst Koegler. The earlier volume should not be discarded, as it remains a valuable resource.

Fifty Contemporary Choreographers. Martha Bremser, ed. London: Routledge, 1999.

International Dictionary of Ballet. Martha Bremser, ed. Detroit: St. James Press, 1993. 2 vols.

International Dictionary of Modern Dance. Taryn Benbow-Pfaltzgraff, ed. Detroit: St. James Press, 1998.

The International Encyclopedia of Dance. New York: Oxford University Press, 1998. 6 vols. Selma Jeanne Cohen, founding editor; Elizabeth Aldrich, managing editor.

Knowles, Mark. *The Tap Dance Dictionary*. Jefferson, N.C.: McFarland, 1998.

Leiter, Samuel. *New Kabuki Encyclopedia: A Revised Adaptation of Kabuki Jiten*. Westport, Conn.: Greenwood Press, 1997.

Love, Paul. *Modern Dance Terminology*. New Introduction by Eleanor King. Pennington, N.J.: Princeton Book Co., 1997.

Matteo (Vittucii, Matteo Marcellus), with Carola Goya. *The Language of Spanish Dance*. Norman: University of Oklahoma Press, 1993.

Preston-Dunlop, Valerie. *Dance Words: A Dictionary of Western Dance Practice and Research*. Choreography and Dance Studies, Vol. 8. Buffalo, N.Y.: Gordon and Breach/Harwood Academic Publishers, 1995.

Raffe, Walter George. *Dictionary of the Dance*. New York: Barnes, 1964.

Ray, Ollie M. *Encyclopedia of Line Dances: The Steps that Came and Stayed*. Reston, Va.: National Dance Association, 1992.

Ryman, Rhonda. *Dictionary of Classical Ballet Terminology*. London: Royal Academy of Dancing, 1995, 2nd ed. 1997.

Nonprint resources

Video Dictionary of Classical Ballet, prod. and dir. Robert Beck, Transmedia Communications Network in association with the Metropolitan Opera Guild, 270 minutes, distr. Princeton Books Company, 1983. Videocassette.

Vocabulary of classical ballet technique demonstrated by Georgina Parkinson, Kevin McKenzie, Denise Jackson, and Merrill Ashley.

Guides and Handbooks

Balanchine, George, and Francis Mason. *Balanchine's Complete Stories of the Great Ballets.* Rev. ed. Garden City, N.Y.: Doubleday, 1977. 838 pages.

Balanchine, George, and Francis Mason. *101 Stories of the Great Ballets.* New York: Doubleday, 1975.

Beaumont, Cyril W. *Complete Book of Ballets: A Guide to the Principal Ballets of the Nineteenth and Twentieth Centuries.* New York: Grosset and Dunlap, 1938. 900 pages. Rev.ed. 1949; reprint with additions, 1951. Beaumont, Cyril. *Complete Book of Ballets: A Guide to the Principal Ballets of the Nineteenth and Twentieth Centuries.* Rev. ed. London: Putnam, 1956.

———. *Supplement.* 1945. Reprinted 1952.

———. *Ballets of Today.* 2nd Supplement. London: Putnam, 1954.

———. *Ballets Past and Present.* 3rd Supplement. London: Putnam, 1955.

Bopp, Mary S. *Research in Dance: A Guide to Resources.* New York: G.K. Hall, 1994.

Dance Magazine College Guide: A Directory of Dance in North American Colleges and Universities. Oakland, Calif.: Dance Magazine. New edition produced in about five year intervals.

Greskovic, Robert. *Ballet 101: A Complete Guide to Learning and Loving the Ballet.* New York: Hyperion, 1998.

McDonagh, Don. *Don McDonagh's Complete Guide to Modern Dance.* New York: Doubleday, 1976.

National Dance Association. *National Standards for Dance Education: What Every Young American Should Know and Be Able to Do in Dance.* Pennington, N.J.: Princeton Book Co., 1994.

Poor Dancer's Almanac: Managing Life and Work in the Performing Arts.. Compiled by the Dance Theater Workshop, David R. White, Lise Friedman, and Tia Tibbitts Levinson., eds. Durham, N.C.: Duke University Press, 1993.

Schlundt, Christena L. *Dance in the Musical Theater: Jerome Robbins and His Peers: A Guide.* New York: Garland, 1989.

Spain, Louise, ed. *Dance On Camera: A Guide to Dance Films and Videos.* Lanham, Md., and London: Scarecrow Press; New York: Neal-Schuman Publishers, Inc., 1998. Supercedes an earlier edition titled: *Dance Film and Video Guide.* Diedre Towers, compiler. Princeton, N.J.: Princeton Book Co., 1991.

Directories/Annuals/Yearbooks

Most of this material is time-sensitive, and is now published online. Included is a suggested list of sources reflective of this technological change in publishing.

Print resources

Directory of Doctoral Programs in Theatre Studies, Performance Studies, and Dance: U.S.A. and Canada. 2nd ed. Editors: Peter A. Davis, Thomas Postlewait. Providence: American Society for Theatre Research, 1996.

Performing Arts Yearbook for Europe. 1st ed. (1991)– London: Arts Publishing International, 1990– . Annual. 4th ed., 1994.

SIBMAS International Directory of Performing Arts Collections. 1st ed. Haslemere, England: Emmett Publishing, 1996.

    Complete revision of *Performing Arts Libraries and Museums of the World.* 3rd ed., 1984.

Stern's Performing Arts Directory. Oakland, Calif.: Dance Magazine, Inc. Annual publication, first appeared in 1989.

Related Reference Works

The following titles cover many dance-related areas and are recommended for inclusion in dance reference collections. Included is a title listing of related reference works available in electronic format.

Print resources

Barba, Eugenio, and Nicola Savarese. *The Dictionary of Theatre Anthropology: The Secret Art of the Performer.* New York: Routledge, 1991. 272 pages.

Highfill, Philip H., Jr. *A Biographical Dictionary of Actors, Actresses, Musicians, Dancers, Managers, and Other Stage Personnel in London 1660–1800.* 16 vols. Carbondale: University of Southern Illinois Press, 1993.

Mapp, Edward. *Directory of Blacks in the Performing Arts.* 2nd ed. Metuchen, N.J.: Scarecrow Press, 1990.

The New York Public Library Performing Arts Desk Reference. New York: Macmillan, 1994.

Odell, George C. D. *Annals of the New York Stage.* New York: Columbia University Press, 1927–1949.

Steinfirst, Susan. *Folklore and Folklife: A Guide to English–Language Reference Sources.* New York: Garland Publishing, 1992. (Garland Folklore Bibliographies, v. 16)

Nonprint resources

Dance On Disc: The Complete Catalog of the Dance Collection of the New York Public Library. New York: G.K. Hall, 199?– . Annual. CD-ROM.

Officer, Jill. *The Encyclopedia of Theatre Dance in Canada.* Toronto: Dance Collection Danse, 1990. CD-ROM.

Electronic Indexes

Art Abstracts
Bibliographic Guide to Dance
Film Literature Index
Humanities Abstracts
International Index to Dance Periodicals
International Theatre Index
Music Index
RILM

The history of dance has been written within and across the disciplines of the arts and humanities, in a variety of published works, representing different aspects of dance history. This section includes volumes that contain comprehensive overviews of the history of dance, from different perspectives within the field. Specific historical accounts of elements of dance history can be found within all of the other sections of this bibliography.

Print resources

Anderson, Jack. *Ballet and Modern Dance: A Concise History.* Pennington,N.J.: Princeton Book Co., 1986.

Au, Susan. *Ballet and Modern Dance.* London and New York: Thames and Hudson, 1988.

Carreiro, Assis. *Ballet and Dance in the 1940's: An Historical Retrospective: The War Years and Beyond.* Birmingham, England: DanceXchange, 1995.

Clarke, Mary and Clement Crisp. *The History of Dance.* New York, Crown Publishers, 1981.

Dance as a Theatre Art: Source Readings in Dance History from 1581 to the Present. Selma Jeanne Cohen, ed. New York: Dodd, Mead, 1974 (reprint, with a new selection by Robbins, Harper and Row, New York, 1976; Dance Books Ltd., London, 1977); 2nd ed., Princeton Book Co., Princeton, N.J., 1992.

Dance History: An Introduction. Janet Adshead-Lansdale and June Lawson, eds. 2nd ed. London; New York: Routledge, 1994.

De Mille, Agnes. *The Book of the Dance.* New York: Golden Press, 1963.

Fonteyn, Margot. *The Magic of Dance.* New York: Knopf, 1979.

Kirstein, Lincoln. *Dance: A Short History of Classic Theatrical Dancing.* Princeton, N.J.: Princeton Book Co., 1987.

Kraus, Richard G., and Sarah Chapman Hilsendager. *History of the Dance in Art and Education.* 2d. ed. Englewood Cliffs, N.J. : Prentice-Hall, 1980, c. 1981.

Martin, John Joseph. *Introduction to the Dance.* Brooklyn: Dance Horizons, 1965.

Sachs, Curt. *World History of the Dance.* New York: Bonanza Books: 1937. (Other editions: New York: Seven Arts, 1937; New York:

W.W. Norton, 1937 and 1963; London: Allen and Unwin Ltd.,
1938; New York: Seven Arts, 1952.

Sorell, Walter. *Dance in Its Time: The Emergence of an Art Form.* New
York: Doubleday, 1981. Reprint: Columbia University Press,
1986.

Nonprint resources

Dancing, prod. WNET and BBC-TV, dir. Rhoda Grauer. 60 minutes
each of 8 programs, distr. Kultur, home Vision, Facets, 1993, 8
videocassettes.

> Exploration of dance as a form of communication and
> expression in a variety of cultures. The programs were
> photographed in eighteen countries.

JVC video anthology of world music and dance. Editor, Fujii Tomoaki ;
assistant editors, Omori Yasuhiro, Sakurai Tetsuo; in collaboration with the National Museum of Ethnology, Osaka; Tokyo;
JVC, Victor Company of Japan; Cambridge, Mass.: distributed
by Rounder Records, 1990

> 30 videocassettes (VHS) and 9 vols. text with maps.

Dance Biographies and Autobiographies

Biographical writing in dance represents an enormous portion of the published literature. Not all biographies written on dancers and dance groups have been included in this section. Selection was based on the comprehensivness of the material and its significance to the field. While the state of dance biography continues to grow and improve, there are still many important figures for which full-length biographical works have not yet appeared. While many of these titles in this list are out of print, they are included, as they still remain the standard and/or only biographical work on important dance figures. Videotapes and films are listed, as in some cases, they are the superior or sole source. The arrangement is alphabetical by subject, and is inclusive of all formats within the sub-sections of Group Biographies and Individuals. Additionally, *Current Biography* regularly features profiles of dancers and choreographers.

Group Biographies

Dance: Four Pioneers, prod. Jac Venza for WNET/13, dir. Charles S. Dubin, distr. Indiana University, University of Minnesota, 30 minutes, 1966. Videocassette.

> The film introduces the modern dance pioneers associated with Bennington College in the 1930s: Martha Graham, Doris Humphrey, Charles Weidman, and Hanya Holm.

Fifty Contemporary Choreographers. Martha Bremser, ed. London: Routledge, 1999.

> Among the choreographers are Stephen Petronio, Twyla Tharp, Trisha Brown, and William Forsythe.

Gruen, John. *People Who Dance: 22 Dancers Tell Their Own Stories*. Pennington, N.J.: Dance Horizons Books : Princeton Book Co., c.1988.

Guest, Ivor. *The Romantic Ballet in Paris*. London: I. Pittman, 1966; Middletown, Conn.: Wesleyan University Press, 1966; London: Dance Books, 1980.

Livingston, Lili Cockerille. *American Indian Ballerinas*. Norman: University of Oklahoma Press, 1997.

> Biographies of Marjorie Tallchief, Maria Tallchief, Yvonne Chouteau, and Rosella Hightower.

Newman, Barbara. *Striking a Balance: Dancers Talk About Dancing.* Boston: Houghton-Mifflin, 1982.
> Interviews with 24 ballet dancers.

Perron, Wendy ed. *Judson Dance Theater: 1962-1966.* Bennington, Vt.: Bennington College, 1981.

Prevots, Naima. *Dancing in the Sun: Hollywood Choreographers, 1915–1937.* Ann Arbor, Mich.: UMI Research Press, 1987.
> Among the choreographers are Norma Gould, Adolf Bolm, Benjamin Zemach, and Ernest Belcher.

Souritz, Elizabeth. *Soviet Choreographers in the 1920s.* Translated from the Russian by Lynn Visson; Edited, with additional translation by Sally Banes. Durham: Duke University Press, 1990.

Individuals

Ailey, Alvin.
> Ailey, Alvin. *Revelations: The Autobiography of Alvin Ailey.* Secaucus, N.J.: Carol Publishing Group, 1994.
> Dunning, Jennifer. *Alvin Ailey: A Life in Dance.* Reading, Mass.: Addison Wesley Longman, 1996.

Allan, Maud.
> Cherniavsky, Felix. *The Salome Dancer: The Life and Times of Maud Allan.* Toronto: McClelland & Stewart, 1991.

Alonso, Alicia.
> Hechavarría, María del Carmen. *Alicia Alonso: Más Allá de la Téchnica.* Valencia, Spain: Universidad Politécnica de Valencia, 1998.

La Argentina
> Bennahum, Ninochka. *La Argentina.* Hanover, N.H.: University Press of New England, 2000.

Arpino, Gerald
> Anawalt, Sasha. *The Joffrey Ballet: Robert Joffrey and the Making of an American Dance Company.* New York: Scribner, 1996.

Includes the biography of Gerald Arpino, the Joffrey Ballet's principal choreographer and current artistic director.

Ashley, Merrill.

Ashley, Merrill. *Dancing for Balanchine*. New York: Dutton, 1984.

Ashton, Frederick.

Kavanagh, Julie. *Secret Muses: The Life of Frederick Ashton*. New York: Pantheon Books, 1996.

Vaughan, David. *Frederick Ashton and His Ballets*. New York: Knopf, 1977.

Astaire, Fred.

Astaire, Fred. *Steps in Time*. New York: Da Capo, 1981.

Baker, Josephine.

Baker, Jean-Claude and Chris Chase. *Josephine: The Hungry Heart*. New York: Random House, 1994.

The Josephine Baker Story, dir. Ralph Gibson, 129 minutes, 1990, distr. HBO Home Video, Facets. Videocassette.

Rose, Phyllis. *Jazz Cleopatra: Josephine Baker in Her Time*. New York: Doubleday, 1989.

Balanchine, George.

Buckle, Richard, in collaboration with John Taras. *George Balanchine: Ballet Master*. New York: Random House, 1988.

Kirstein, Lincoln. *Portrait of Mr. B*. New York: A Ballet Society Book/Viking, 1984.

Mason, Francis. *I Remember Balanchine: Recollections of the Ballet Master by Those Who Knew Him*. New York: Doubleday, 1991.

McDonagh, Don. *George Balanchine*. Boston: Twayne Publishers, 1983.

Taper, Bernard. *Balanchine*. New York: Harper and Row, 1963, rev. ed. published as *Balanchine: A Biography*. Berkeley: University of California Press, 1996.

Dancing for Mr. B.: Six Balanchine Ballerinas, prod. and dir. Anne Belle, distr. Direct Cinema, WarnerVision Entertainment, Viewfinders, Dance Horizons, Facets, 90 minutes, 1989. Videocassette.
> Participants are Maria Tallchief, Mary Ellen Moylan, Melissa Hayden, Allegra Kent, Merrill Ashley, and Darci Kistler.

Baryshnikov, Mikhail.
> Baryshnikov, Mikhail, text, with photography by Martha Swope. *Baryshnikov at Work: Mikhail Baryshnikov Discusses His Roles*. Edited and introduced by Charles Engell France. New York: Knopf, 1976.
> Smakov, Gennady. *Baryshnikov: From Russia to the West*. New York: Farrar Straus and Giroux, 1981.

Bausch, Pina.
> Servos, Norbert. *Pina Bausch Wuppertal Dance Theater: Or the Art of Training a Goldfish—Excursions into Dance*. Translated by Patricia Stadié. Cologne: Ballett-Bühnen Verlag, 1984.

Berk, Fred.
> Ingber, Judith Brin. *Victory Dances: The Story of Fred Berk, a Modern Day Jewish Dancing Master*. Tel Aviv: Israel Dance Library, 1985.

Bonfanti, Maria.
> Barker, Barbara. *Ballet or Ballyhoo: The American Careers of Maria Bonfanti, Rita Sangalli and Giuseppina Morlacchi*. New York: Dance Horizons, 1984.

Bournonville, August.
> Bournonville, August. *My Theatre Life*. Translated from Danish by Patricia N. McAndrew. Middletown, Conn.: Wesleyen University Press, 1979.

Bruhn, Erik.
> Gruen, John. *Erik Bruhn: Danseur Noble*. New York: Viking, 1979.

Bujones, Fernando.
>Bujones, Fernando. *Fernando Bujones.* Rio de Janeiro: Imprinta Gráfica e Editora, 1984. Bilingual: Spanish/ English.

Camargo, Marie,
>Montagu-Nathan, M. *Mlle. Camargo.* Artists of the Dance. London: British-continental Press, 1932.

Castle, Vernon and Irene.
>Castle, Irene. *Castles in the Air.* Garden City, New York: Doubleday, 1958.

Cecchetti, Enrico.
>Beaumont, Cyril W. *Enrico Cecchetti: A Memoir.* London: C.W. Beaumont, 1929.
>Racster, Olga. *The Master of the Russian Ballet: The Memoirs of Cav. Enrico Cecchetti.* Introduction by Anna Pavlova. London: Hutchinson & Co., 1922; reprint New York: Da Capo Press, 1978.

Cerrito, Fanny.
>Guest, Ivor. *Fanny Cerrito: The Life of a Romantic Ballerina.* 2nd rev. ed. London: Dance Books, 1974.

Christensen Brothers
>Sowell, Debra. *The Christensen Brothers: An American Dance Epic.* Amsterdam: Harwood Academic Publishers, 1998.

Cocteau, Jean
>Steegmuller, Francis. *Cocteau, a Biography.* Boston: Little, Brown, 1970.
>>As an important collaborator in the Diaghilev Ballets Russes, Cocteau's biography is informative about the artistic life of Paris in the early twentieth century.

Cole, Jack.
>Loney, Glenn Meredith. *Unsung Genius: The Passion of*

Dancer-Choreographer Jack Cole. New York & London: Franklin Watts, 1984.

Cunningham, Merce.
  Cage/Cunningham, dir. Elliot Caplan, distr. Cunningham Dance Foundation, Kultur, Dance Horizons, 95 minutes, 1991. Videocassette.
    Documentary on Merce Cunningham and composer/collaborator John Cage, and their influence on other artists.
  Cunningham, Merce. *The Dancer and the Dance: In Conversation with Jacqueline Lesschaeve.* New York: Marion Boyars, 1985.
  Klosty, James, ed. *Merce Cunningham.* New York: Saturday Review Press, 1975; reprint New York: Proscenium, 1985; and reprint, New York: Limelight, 1986.
  Vaughan, David. *Merce Cunningham: Fifty Years.* New York: Aperture, 1997.

Dalcroze, Emile Jaques.
  Spector, Irwin. *Rhythm and Life: The Work of Emile Jaques Dalcroze.* Stuyvesant, New York: Pendragon Press, 1990.

Danilova, Alexandra.
  Danilova, Alexandra. *Choura: The Memoirs of Alexandra Danilova.* New York: Knopf, 1986.
  Reflections of a Dancer: Alexandra Danilova, Prima Ballerina Assoluta, prod. and dir. Anne Belle, 52 minutes, 1981, distr. Direct Cinema. Videocassette.

De Mille, Agnes.
  Easton, Carol. *No Intermissions: The Life of Agnes de Mille.* New York, London, Toronto: Little Brown and Company, 1996.
  De Mille, Agnes. *Dance to the Piper and All the Way Home: A Two-Part Autobiography.* New York: Da Capo Press, 1979.

De Valois, Ninette.
>De Valois, Ninette. *Come Dance With Me.* New York: World,
>1958.
>Walker, Kathrine Sorley . *Ninette de Valois: Idealist Without
>Illusions.* With contributions by Dame Ninette. London:
>Hamish Hamilton, 1987.

Diaghilev, Serge.
>Buckle, Richard. *Diaghilev.* New York: Simon & Schuster,
>1984.
>Drummond, John. *Speaking of Diaghilev.* London, Boston:
>Faber and Faber, 1997.
>MacDonald, Nesta. *Diaghilev Observed by Critics in England
>and the United States, 1911–1929.* New York: Dance
>Horizons, 1975.

Didelot, Charles-Louis.
>Swift, Mary Grace. *A Loftier Flight; The Life and
>Accomplishments of Charles-Louis Didelot,
>Balletmaster.* Middletown, Conn.: Wesleyan Uni-
>versity Press, 1974.

Duncan, Isadora.
>Blair, Fredrika. *Isadora: Portrait of the Artist as a Woman.* New
>York: McGraw-Hill, 1986.
>Daly, Ann. *Done into Dance: Isadora Duncan in
>America.* Bloomington: Indiana University Press,
>1995.
>Duncan, Isadora. *My Life.* Garden City, N.Y. Garden City
>Publishing Company, c. 1927.
>Loewenthal, Lillian. *The Search for Isadora: The Legend &
>Legacy of Isadora Duncan.* Princeton, N.J.: Princeton Book
>Company, 1993.
>Steegmuller, Francis. *Your Isadora.* New York: Random
>House and New York Public Library, 1974.

Dunham, Katherine.
>Beckford, Ruth. *Katherine Dunham, a Biography.* New York:
>Dekker, 1979.

Donloe, Darlene. *Katherine Dunham: Dancer and Choreographer*. Los Angeles: Holloway House, 1993.

Haskins, James. *Katherine Dunham*. New York: Coward, McCann & Geoghegan, 1982.

Elssler, Fanny.

Guest, Ivor. *Fanny Elssler*. Middletown, Conn.: Wesleyan University Press, 1970.

Farrell, Suzanne.

Farrell, Suzanne, with Toni Bentley. *Holding On to the Air: An Autobiography*. New York: Summit Books, 1990.

Suzanne Farrell: Elusive Muse, prod. Anne Belle and Catherine Tambini, dir. Anne Belle and Deborah Dickson, 90 minutes, 1996, distr. WNET Video Distribution. Videocassette.

Fokine, Michel.

Fokine, Michel. *Memoirs of A Ballet Master*. Boston: Little, Brown, 1961.

Horwitz, Dawn Lille. *Michel Fokine*. Boston: Twayne Publishers, 1985.

Fonteyn, Margot.

Fonteyn, Margot. *Autobiography*. New York: Alfred A. Knopf, 1976.

Money, Keith. *Fonteyn: The Making of a Legend*. New York: Reynall, 1974.

Fosse, Bob.

Gottfried, Martin. *All His Jazz—The Life and Death of Bob Fosse*. New York: Bantam Books, 1990.

Grubb, Kevin Boyd. *Razzle Dazzle: The Life and Work of Bob Fosse*. New York: St. Martin's Press, 1989.

Fuller, Loie.

Current, Richard Nelson. *Loie Fuller, Goddess of Light*. Boston: Northeastern University Press, 1997.

Sommer, Sally and Margaret Harris. *La Loie: The Life and Art of Loie Fuller*. New York: Putnam, 1986.

Geva, Tamara.
> Geva, Tamara. *Split Seconds: A Remembrance.* New York: Harper & Row, 1972.

Glover, Savion.
> Glover, Savion and Bruce Weber. *Savion!: My Life in Tap.* New York: W. Morrow, 2000.

Graham, Martha.
> De Mille, Agnes. *Martha: The Life and Work of Martha Graham.* New York: Random House, 1991.
>
> Graham, Martha. *Blood Memory.* New York: Doubleday, 1991.
>
> Leatherman, Leroy. *Martha Graham: Portrait of the Lady as an Artist.* Photographs by Martha Swope. New York: Knopf, 1966.
>
> McDonagh, Don. *Martha Graham.* New York: Praeger, 1973.

Harkness, Rebekah
> Unger, Craig. *Blue Blood.* New York: Morrow, 1988.
>> Biography of the heiress who founded the Harkness Ballet and the Harkness Foundation for the Arts.

Holm, Hanya.
> Sorell, Walter. *Hanya Holm: The Biography of an Artist.* Middletown, Conn: Wesleyan University Press, 1969; reprint 1979.
>
> *Hanya: Portrait of a Dance Pioneer,* prod. Nancy Mason Hauser and Marily Christofori, dir. John Ittelson, distr. Dance Horizons, 55 minutes, 1984. Videocassette.

Horst, Louis.
> Soares, Janet Mansfield. *Louis Horst: Musician in a Dancer's World.* Durham: Duke University Press, 1992.
>> On Horst's musical collaboration with Denishawn and Martha Graham, and his choreography workshops at Juilliard and the American Dance Festival.

Horton, Lester.
>   Warren, Larry. *Lester Horton: Modern Dance Pioneer.* New
>   York & Basel: Marcel Dekker, 1977; reprint Princeton,
>   N.J. Princeton Book Company, Publishers, 1991.

Humphrey, Doris.
>   Humphrey, Doris. *Doris Humphrey: An Artist First.* Edited by
>   Selma Jeanne Cohen. Middletown, Conn.: Wesleyan
>   University Press, 1972.
>   Siegel, Marcia B. *Days on Earth: The Dance of Doris
>   Humphrey.* New Haven, Conn. & London: Yale Univer-
>   sity Press, 1987; reprint Durham: Duke University Press,
>   1992.

Ito, Michio.
>   Caldwell, Helen. *Michio Ito: The Dancer and His Dances.*
>   Berkeley: University of California Press, 1977.

Ivanov, Lev.
>   Wiley, Roland John *The Life and Ballets of Lev Ivanov:
>   Choreographer of the Nutcracker and Swan Lake.* New York:
>   Oxford University Press, 1997.

Jamison, Judith.
>   Jamison, Judith, and Howard Kaplan. *Dancing Spirit: An
>   Autobiography.* New York: Doubleday, 1993.

Joffrey, Robert.
>   Anawalt, Sasha. *The Joffrey Ballet: Robert Joffrey and the
>   Making of an American Dance Company.* New York:
>   Scribner, 1996.

Jones, Bill T.
>   Jones, Bill T., and Arnie Zane. *Body Against Body: The
>   Dance and Other Collaborations.* Elizabeth Zimmer and
>   Susan Quasha, eds. Barrytown, N.Y.: Station Hill
>   Press, 1989.
>   Jones, Bill T. with Peggy Gillespie. *Last Night on Earth.* New
>   York: Pantheon Books, 1995.

Jooss, Kurt.

> Coton, A.V. *The New Ballet: Kurt Jooss and His Work.* London: Dennis Dobson, 1946.
>
> Markard, Anna and Hermann Markard. *Jooss.* Cologne: Balett-Vuhnen Verlag, 1985. Bilingual: English/German.

Karsavina, Tamara.

> Karsavina, Tamara. *Theatre Street.* Rev. and enl. Ed. London: Constable, 1948.

Kaye, Danny

> Gottfried, Martin. *Nobody's Fool: The Lives of Danny Kaye.* New York: Simon and Schuster, 1994.

Kelly, Gene.

> Hirschhorn, Clive. *Gene Kelly: A Biography.* 2nd ed. New York: St. Martin's, 1984.
>
> Yudkoff, Alvin. *Gene Kelly: A Life of Dance and Dreams.* New York: Watson-Guptil Publications, 2000.

Kent, Allegra

> Kent, Allegra. *Once a Dancer.* New York: St. Martin's Press, 1997.

Kirkland, Gelsey.

> Kirkland, Gelsey, with Greg Lawrence. *Dancing on My Grave.* Garden City, N.Y.: Doubleday, 1986.

Koner, Pauline.

> Koner, Pauline. *Solitary Song.* Durham: Duke University Press, 1989.

Laban, Rudolf von.

> Laban, Rudolf von. *A Life for Dance: Reminiscences.* With drawings by the author. Translated and annotated by Lisa Ullmann. New York, Theatre Arts Books, 1975.

Limón, José.

> *José Limón: An Unfinished Memoir.* Edited by Lynn Garafola;

introduction by Deborah Jowitt. Middletown, Conn.:
Wesleyan University Press; Hanover, N.H.: University
Press of New England, 1999.

Louis, Murray.
> Louis, Murray. *Murray Louis on Dance*. Chicago: A Cappella
> Books, 1992.

MacMillan, Kenneth.
> Thorpe, Edward. *Kenneth MacMillan: The Man and the
> Ballets*. London: Hamish Hamilton, 1985.

Makarova, Natalia.
> Makarova, Natalia. *A Dance Autobiography*. Introduced and
> edited by Gennady Smakov; photos. by Dina Makarova
> and others. New York, Knopf, 1979.

Martins, Peter.
> Martins, Peter. *Far from Denmark*. With Robert Cornfield.
> Boston: Little, Brown, c. 1982.

Massine, Leonide.
> Garcia-Marquez, Vicente. *Massine: A Biography*. New York :
> Knopf, 1995.
> Massine, Leonide. *My Life in Ballet*. Edited by Phyllis
> Hartnoll and Robert Rubens. With a catalogue of ballets
> by Phyllis Hartnoll. London: Macmillan; New York: St.
> Martin's Press, 1968.

Miller, Norma.
> Miller, Norma with Evette Jensen. *Swinging at the Savoy:
> The Memoir of a Jazz Dancer*. Philadelphia: Temple
> University Press, 1996.

Monk, Meredith.
> Jowitt, Deborah, ed. *Meredith Monk*. Baltimore: Johns
> Hopkins University Press, 1997.
>> An anthology of critical writing about Monk's work
>> and extensive interviews with her.

Morris, Mark.
> Acocella, Joan Ross. *Mark Morris*. New York: Farrar Straus
> Giroux, 1993.

Mumaw, Barton.
> Sherman, Jane and Barton Mumaw. *Barton Mumaw, Dancer:*
> *From Denishawn to Jacob's Pillow and Beyond*. Hanover,
> N.H.: Wesleyan University Press, 2000.

Nicholas Brothers.
> Hill, Constance Valis. *Brotherhood in Rhythm: The Jazz Tap*
> *Dancing of the Nicholas Brothers*. New York: Oxford
> University Press, 2000.

Nijinska, Bronislava.
> Nijinska, Bronislava. *Bronislava Nijinska: Early Memoirs*.
> Translated and edited by Irina Nijinska and Jean Rawlinson.
> New York: Holt, Rinehart and Winston, 1981.
> *Nijinska: A Legend in Dance*, prod. and dir. Linda Schaller,
> distr. KQED-TV, 58 minutes, 1988. Videocassette.

Nijinsky, Vasily.
> Buckle, Richard. *Nijinsky*. London: Weidenfield &
> Nicholson, 1979.
> Kirstein, Lincoln. *Nijinsky Dancing*. New York, Knopf, 1975.
> Krasovskaia, Vera. *Nijinsky*. New York: Schirmer/Macmillan, 1979.
> Nijinsky, Vaslav. *The Diary of Vaslav Nijinsky*. Edited and
> with an introduction by Joan Acocella. New York: Farrar,
> Straus and Giroux, 1999.
> Ostwald, Peter. *Nijinsky: A Leap into Madness*. New York:
> Carol Publishing Group, 1991.

Noverre, Jean Georges.
> Lynham, Deryck. *The Chevalier Noverre: Father of Modern*
> *Ballet, a Biography*. London: Dance Books, 1972.

Nureyev, Rudolf.
> Bland, Alexander. *Fonteyn and Nureyev: The Story of a*
> *Partnership*. New York: Times Books, 1979.

Nureyev, prod. and dir. Patricia Foy, distr. Home Vision, 90 minutes, 1991. Videocassette.

Solway, Diane. *Nureyev: His Life.* London: Weidenfeld and Nicolson, 1998; New York: William Morrow, 1998.

Osato, Sono.

Osato, Sono. *Distant Dances.* New York: Knopf, 1980.

Page, Ruth.

Martin, John Joseph. *Ruth Page: An Intimate Biography.* New York & Basel: Marcel Dekker, 1977.

Pavlova, Anna.

Money, Keith. *Anna Pavlova: Her Life and Her Art.* New York: Knopf, 1982.

Perrot, Jules.

Guest, Ivor. *Jules Perrot: Master of the Romantic Ballet.* New York: Dance Horizons, 1984.

Petipa, Marius.

Petipa, Marius. *Russian Ballet Master: The Memoirs of Marius Petipa.* Translated by Helen Whittaker. Edited by Lillian Moore. London: Adam & Charles Black, 1958.

Plisetskaya, Maya.

Plisetskaya Dances, prod. Central Soviet Film Studio, dir. Vasili Katanyan, distrs. Kultur, Dance Horizons, Home Vision, 70 minutes, 1964. Videocassette.

Roslavleva, Natalia. *Maya Plisetskaya.* Moscow: Foreign Language Publishing House, 1956.

Rambert, Marie.

Rambert, Marie. *Quicksilver: The Autobiography of Marie Rambert.* New York: St. Martin's Press, 1972.

Rainer, Yvonne.

Rainer, Yvonne. *Work 1961-73.* Halifax: Nova Scotia College of Art and Design, 1974.

Robbins, Jerome.

>Conrad, Christine. *Jerome Robbins: That Broadway Man, That Ballet Man.* London: Booth-Clibborn Editions, distr. Harry N. Abrams and Time Warner Trade Publishing, 2000.
>>A study of Robbins' life and career based on photographic documentation.

Shawn, Ted.

>Shawn, Ted, with Gray Poole. *One Thousand and One Night Stands.* Garden City, N.Y.: Doubleday, 1960.

Sherman, Jane.

>Sherman, Jane. *Soaring: The Diary and Letters of a Denishawn Dancer in the Far East 1925–1926.* Middletown, Conn.: Wesleyan University Press, 1976.

Sokolow, Anna.

>Warren, Larry. *Anna Sokolow: The Rebellious Spirit.* Princeton, N.J.: Princeton Book Co., 1991.

St. Denis, Ruth.

>Kendall, Elizabeth. *Where She Danced: The Birth of American Art-Dance.* Berkeley: University of California Press, 1984.
>Shelton, Suzanne. *Divine Dancer: A Biography of Ruth St. Denis.* Garden City, N.J.: Doubleday, 1981.
>St. Denis, Ruth. *An Unfinished Life.* New York: Dance Horizons, 1969.

Taglioni, Marie.

>Levinson, André. *Marie Taglioni (1804–1884).* London: Dance Books, 1977.

Tallchief, Maria.

>Tallchief, Maria with Larry Kaplan. *Maria Tallchief: America's Prima Ballerina.* New York: Henry Holt, 1997.

Taylor, Paul.

>Taylor, Paul. *Private Domain.* New York: Knopf, 1987.

Tharp, Twyla.
> Tharp, Twyla. *Push Comes to Shove: An Autobiography.* New York: Bantam Books, 1992.

Tudor, Antony.
> Chazin-Bennahum, Judith. *The Ballets of Antony Tudor. Studies in Psyche and Satire.* New York: Oxford University Press, 1994.
> Perlmutter, Donna. *Shadowplay: The Life of Antony Tudor.* New York: Viking, 1991.

Ulanova, Galina.
> Kahn, Albert E. *Days with Ulanova.* New York: Simon and Schuster, 1962.

Villella, Edward.
> Villella, Edward with Larry Kaplan. *Prodigal Son: Dancing for Balanchine in a World of Pain and Magic.* New York: Simon & Schuster, 1992.

Weaver, John.
> Weaver, John. *The Life and Works of John Weaver: An Account of his Life, Writings and Theatrical Productions, with an Annotated Reprint of His Complete Publications.* New York: Dance Horizons, 1985.

Weidman, Charles.
> *Charles Weidman: On His Own*, prod. Charles Weidman Dance Foundation, dir. Virginia Brooks and Janet Mendelsohn, distr. Dance Horizons, 59 minutes, 1990. Videocassette.

Wigman, Mary.
> Manning, Susan. *Ecstasy and the Demon: Feminism and Nationalism in the Dances of Mary Wigman.* Berkeley: University of California Press, 1993.
> *Mary Wigman: When the Fire Dances Between the Two Poles*, prod. and dir. Allegra Fuller Snyder and Annette MacDonald, distr. Dance Horizons, University of Cali-

fornia Extension Center, 45 minutes, 1982. Videocassette.

Sorell, Walter. *The Mary Wigman Book.* Middletwon, Conn.: Wesleyan University Press, 1973, 1975.

Zucchi, Virginia.

Guest, Ivor. *The Divine Virginia: A Biography of Virginia Zucchi.* New York & Basel: Marcel Dekker, 1977.

DANCE STYLES, FORMS, AND TRADITIONS

The categorization of materials in this section was decided through an analysis of the significance of the grouping, whether it be geographic location, or the specific style by which the style, form or tradition has been most identified in the existing literature. Recent scholarship has heightened the awareness of the field of dance as to the cultural diversity within the field, resulting in the emergence of a more defined body of literature. As the literature continues to evolve, this classification system will be revised to adapt to new standards and structures in the fields of dance and library science. In addition to the titles suggested in this section, students and researchers will benefit greatly by consulting articles listed in the Land and Peoples section in the Synoptic Outline of Contents in the *International Encyclopedia of Dance*. It should be noted that choreographers, dancers, and viewers of dance, as well as those who study and write about dance are culturally based individuals who function within cultural conventions and aesthetic systems. Cultural and academic differences must be considered when reading dance literature. See also the sections on Dance Ethnology and the Anthropology of Dance, and Dance Theory for additional works and perspectives.

Geographical Traditions
AFRICA
The two major cultural regions of Africa are considered to be North Africa and Sub-Saharan Africa. North Africa includes western traditions of the Maghreb (Libya, Tunisia, Algeria, Morocco), the Berbers, and the eastern Arabic influenced traditions of Egypt. Sub-Saharan African traditions are often grouped into three regions: Central and East Africa, West Africa, and Southern Africa. Consult the periodical literature and conference proceedings to supplement this listing. See also the section on Mediterranean and Near-East, for publications that represent the dance which has been identified as specific to those regions. See also the sections on African American Dance and African Carribean Dance for works representing African traditions and influences that have been identified under these headings in the literature. See also the sections on Dance Ethnology and the Anthropology

of Dance, Sacred and Liturgical Dance, and Dance Theory for supplemental literature.

Print resources

African Dance: An Artistic, Historical, and Philosophical Inquiry. Edited by Kariamu Welsh-Asante. Trenton, N.J.: Africa World Press, 1996.
 Collection of essays on African dance in Africa and the Americas.

Ajayi, Omofolabo S. *Yoruba Dance: The Semiotics of Movement and Yoruba Body Attitude in a Nigerian Culture.* Trenton, N.J. : Africa World Press, c.1998.

Asante, Kariamu Welsh. See under Welsh-Asante, Kariamu.

Drewal. M. T. *Yoruba Ritual: Performers, Play, Agency.* Bloomington: University of Indiana Press, 1992.

Emery, Lynne Fauley. *Black Dance: From 1619 to Today.* 2nd. rev. ed. Pennington , N.J.: Princeton Book Co., 1988.
 Foreword by Katherine Dunham. Second edition includes a new chapter by Brenda Dixon-Stowell.

The Spirit's Dance in Africa: Evolution, Transformation, and Continuity in Sub-Sahara. Edited by Esther A. Dagan with an introduction by Simon Ottenberg. Westmount, QC, Canada: Galerie Amrad African Arts Publications, 1997.
 Collection of essays, including historical and anthropological perspectives with many illustrations, focusing on central Africa.

Thompson, Robert Farris. *African Art in Motion; Icon and Act in the Collection of Katherine Coryton White.* Los Angeles: University of California Press, 1974.

———. *Flash of the Spirit: African and Afro-American Art and Philosophy.* New York: Random House, 1983.

Welsh-Asante, Kariamu. *The African Aesthetic: Keeper of the Traditions.* Westport, Conn.: Greenwood Press, 1993.

———. *Umfundalai: An African Dance Technique.* Lawrenceville, N.J.: African World Press, 1995.

———. *Zimbabwe Dance: Rhythmic Forces, Ancestral Voices—An Aesthetic Analysis.* Trenton, N.J.: Africa World Press, 2000.

Nonprint resources

Chuck Davis: Dancing through West Africa. Produced by Gorham Kindem and Jane Desmond; director and cinematographer,

Gorham Kindem. New York, N.Y. : Filmakers Library, c.1986.
Videocassette.

Dances of Southern Africa. Produced, directed and filmed by Gei
Zantzinger. Produced in cooperation with the University-
Museum of the University of Pennsylvania. University Park,
Penn.: Pennyslvania State University, 1973. Narration by Hugh
Tracey with Andrew Tracey.

*JVC/Smithsonian Folkways Video Anthology of Music and Dance of
Africa.* Barre, Vt.: Multicultural Media, 1966. 3 videocassettes.

Kémoko Sano Teaches African Dance from the Republic of Guinea.
Scarsdale, N.Y.: Sano Videos, c.1991. Videocassette.

AMERICAS

Studies of North American dance range from descriptive surveys to
in-depth analyses. To date there are more articles and studies of
specific areas and groups than general descriptions and monographs
on North American dance. For representations of specific forms,
styles and traditions within the Americas, see also the sections on
Latin American Dance and African American Dance, African Caribbean Dance, Ballet, Modern and Postmodern Dance, Jazz Dance, Tap
Dance, and Variety Dance. The perspectives of researchers and
writers have grown and changed, as has the field of dance anthropology and ethnology. Also the dance forms themselves continue to
change in contemporary dance phenomena, and as the traditional
cultures merge with those of immigrants from Europe, Asia and
Africa. This has resulted in the representation of several different
points of view within the literature. See also the sections on Dance
Ethnology and the Anthropology of Dance, European and American Social Dance Traditions, Sacred and Liturgical Dance, as well as
the section on Dance Theory for related works.

North America

The *International Encyclopedia of Dance* (1998) overview article,
"Native American Dance" and related articles on dances of specific
tribes are also useful as a starting point.

Print resources

Kurath, Gertrude Prokosch. *Dance and Song Rituals of Six Nations
Reserve, Ontario.* Ottawa: National Museum of Canada, 1968.

Savigliano, Marta. *Tango and the Political Economy of Passion.* Boulder,
   Colo.: Westview Press, 1995.

Nonprint resources
*JVC/Smithsonian Folkways Video Anthology of Music and Dance of the
   Americas*, volume 6. JVC, Victor Company of Japan; Montpelier,
   Vt.: Multicultural Media, 1995.
      Countries covered on this tape are: Mexico, Nicaragua, Peru,
      and Venezuela

ASIA
This section contains sources synonomous with Asian, East Asian,
South Asian, and Southeast Asian dance traditions. Geographical
areas represented include: China, Japan, Korea, Okinawa, Taiwan,
Afghanistan, Bangladesh, Bhutan, India, Manipur, Sikkim, Pakistan,
Tibet, Cambodia, Indonesia (including Bali and Java), Laos, Malaysia,
Myanmar, and Thailand. Includes many specific Asian dance traditions
such as Kabuki and Bharata Natyam. For specific background informa-
tion, see the *International Encyclopedia of Dance* overview article on
Asian dance, "Asian Dance Traditions," and related articles on countries.
See also the sections on Mediterranian and the Near East, Oceania,
Dance Ethnology and the Anthropology of Dance, as well as the
sections on Sacred and Liturgical Dance, Ballet, Modern and
Postmodern Dance, and Dance Theory for related sources.

Print resources
Adachi, Barbara. *The Voices and Hands of Bunraku.* New York/Tokyo:
   Kodansha, 1978.
Asai, Susan Miyo. *Nomai Dance Drama: A Surviving Spirit of Medi-
   eval Japan.* Westport, Conn.: Greenwood Press, 1999.
Averbuch, Irit. *The Gods Come Dancing: A Study of the Japanese Ritual
   Dance of Yamabushi Kagura.* Ithaca, N.Y.: East Asia Program,
   Cornell University, 1995.
Bandem, I Made, and Fredrik Eugene DeBoer. *Balinese Dance in
   Transition: Kaja and Kelod.* 2nd ed. Kuala Lumper, New York:
   Oxford University Press, 1995. Originally published in 1981
   with the title *Kaja and Kelod: Balinese Dance in Transition.*
Banerji, Sures Chandra. *A Companion to Indian Music and Dance.* Delhi,
   India: Sri Satguru Publications, 1990. (Raga Nrtya series. No.4)

————. *Movement and Mimesis: The Idea of Dance in the Sanskritic Tradition.* Studies of Classical India, vol. 12. Dordrecht; Boston: Kluwer Academic Publishers, 1991.

Butoh: Dance of the Dark Soul. Photographs by Ethan Hoffman, commentaries by Mark Holborn, Yukio Mishima and Tatsumi Hijikata. New York: Aperture, 1987.

Dalby, Liza Crihfield. *Geisha.* Berkeley: University of California Press, 1983.

Dances of ASEAN. Zainal Abiddin Tinggal, general editor. Brunei Darussalam: Association of South East Asian Nations (ASEAN) Committee on Culture and Information, 1998.

    Chapters on Brunei Darussalam, Indonesia, Malaysia, Philippines, Singapore, and Thailand.

Fraleigh, Sandra. *Dancing into Darkness: Butoh, Zen, and Japan.* Pittsburgh: University of Pittsburgh Press, 1999.

Gaston, Anne Marie. *Bharata Natyam: From Temple to Theater.* New Delhi: Manoher, 1996.

Ginn, Victoria. *The Spirited Earth: Dance, Myth, and Ritual from South Asia to the South Pacific.* New York: Rizzoli, 1990.

    Not an anthropological study, but useful for the photographic images.

Gunji, Masakatsu. *Buyo: The Classical Dance of Japan.* New York: Walker/Weatherhill, 1970.

————. *Kabuki.* Photographs by Chiaki Yoshida, introd. by Donald Keene. Tokyo, Palo Alto, Calif.: Kodansha, 1969.

Heyman, Alan. *Dances of the Three-Thousand League Land. Dance Perspectives #19.* Republished in 1966 by Dong-A., Seoul; in 1970 by Johnson Reprint Corp., and in 1981 by Seoul Computer Press.

Kathakali: The Art of the Non-Worldly. D. Appukattan Nair and K. Ayyappapanicker, eds. Bombay: Marg Publications, 1993.

Khokar, Mohan. *Traditions of Indian Classical Dance.* New Delhi: Clarion Books, rev. ed. 1984.

Korean Cultural Heritage. Volume III. Performing Arts. Joungwon Kim, ed. Korea: Korea Foundation. 1997.

Korean Performing Arts. Drama, Dance and Musical Theater. Korean Studies Series No. 6. Seoul: Jipmoondang Publishing Company, 1997.

Kothari, Sunil, ed. *Bharata Natyam.* Bombay: Mary Publications, 1979.

————. *Kathak.* New Delhi: Abhinav Publications, 1989.

————. *Odissi.* Bombay: Marg Publications, 1990.

Lee, Josephine. *Performing Asian American.* Philadelphia: Temple University Press, 1998.

Maruoka, Daiji, and Tatsuo Yoshikoshi. *Noh.* Osaka, Japan: Hoikusha, 1996.

Massey, Reginald, and Jamila Massey. *The Dances of India: A General Guide and A User's Handbook.* Asia Publishing House, 1993.

Miettinen, Jukka O. *Classical Dance and Theatre in South-East Asia.* New York: Oxford University Press, 1993.

Sakakibara, Kiitsu. *Dances of Asia.* Chandigarh, India : Abhishek Publications, 1992.

> Chapters on India, Sri Lanka, Pakistan/Bangladesh, Burma, Thailand, Indonesia, Philippines, Tibet, Korea, China and Okinawa (Japan).

The Traditional Music and Dance of Korea. Seoul: Korean Traditional Performing Arts Centre, 1993.

Nonprint resources

Aak, Korean Court Music and Dance, prod. Beate Gordon for Asia Society, dir. Donald MacLennan, 30 min., distr. Asia Society, 1979. Videocassette.

Circles –Cycles: Kathak Dance, prod. Robert Gottlieb, 28 min., distr. University of California Media Extension Center, 1988. Videocassette.

Kabuki: Classic Theatre of Japan, prod. Kaga Productions, 30 min., distr. Japan Foundation, 1964. Videocassette.

A Life in Two Worlds: Tomasaburo Bando, 20 minutes., prod. Broadcast Programming Center of Japan, distr. Japan Foundation, 1977. Videocassette.

> The world of Kabuki as shown through the career of a contemporary star.

On the Move: Central Ballet of China, prod. Sidney and Mary Yung Kantor and Catherine Tatge, dir. Merrill Brockway, 60 min., distr. Direct Line Cinema, 1987. Videocassette.

EUROPE

Terminology usually associated with European traditional dance include "folk," "traditional," or "national." There are more articles and studies of specific areas and groups than general descriptions, and English language monographs are few. Consult the periodical literature and conference proceedings for more information. For specific background information, see the *International Encyclopedia of Dance* articles on the European peoples with long histories: "Anastenárides," "Basque Dance," "Gypsy Dance," and "Jewish Dance Traditions." Another *International Encyclopedia of Dance* article, "European Traditional Dance," describes forms and functional types: ritual dances, ceremonial dances, participant dances, and presentational-competitive dances. Some attempt to explore the dance of early peoples such as the Celts and Vikings has been made by Curt Sachs in his *World History of the Dance*. For literature specifically on the traditional dance of the United Kingdom and Europe, see the section on European and American Social Dance. For literature on other dance phenomena of the United Kingdom and Europe, see also the sections on Spanish Dance, Sacred and Liturgical Dance, Western European Renaissance and Baroque Dance, Ballet, and Modern and Postmodern Dance. See also Dance Theory for related sources.

Print resources
Torp, Lisbet. *Chain and Round Dance Patterns. A Method for Structural Analysis and Its Application to European Material.* Copenhagen: Museum Tusculanum Press, 1990.

Nonprint resources
These two films are cultural representations of the history of the Gypsies, including Gypsy dance.
Latcho Drom = *Bonne Route*. Presented by Michèle Ray-Gavras ; directed by Tony Gatlif ; produced by Michèle Ray, K.G. Productions. Montréal, Quebec: France Film, 1993. Distributed by New Yorker Films. Videocassette.
The Romany Trail. Produced by Harcourt Films Productions, 1982. Producer/director: Jeremy Marre. Camera: Chris Morphet. Part of the film series Beats of the Heart. Videocassette.

MEDITERRANEAN AND THE NEAR EAST
The majority of the titles in this section are about the form which is variously known as Oriental Dance, Belly Dance, or Middle Eastern Dance. The literature on other dance forms of the Mediterranean

region is not extensive, and offers many opportunities for futher scholarship. The list presents resources on the history and cultural significance of the various forms of Middle Eastern dance, and instructional materials on costuming and dance technique. Some titles on this list may be difficult to obtain, but the authority and value of these materials makes these sources essential. Biographies are useful sources for significant dancers; see the section on Dance Biographies and Autobiographies. See also the sections on Dance Ethnology and the Anthropology of Dance, Ballet, Modern and Postmodern Dance, and Dance Theory for related sources.

Print resources

And, Metin. *A History of Theatre and Popular Entertainment in Turkey.* Ankara: Forum Yayinlari, 1963–1964.

———. *A Pictorial History of Turkish Dancing: From Folk Dancing to WhirlingDervishes—Belly Dancing to Ballet.* Ankara: Dost Yayinlari, 1976.

Berk, Fred. *The Chasidic Dance.* New York: American Zionist Youth Foundation, 1975.

———. *He-rikud: The Jewish Dance.* New York: American Zionist Youth Foundation, 1972.

Buonaventura, Wendy. *Serpent of the Nile.* New York: Interlink Books, 1994.

Carlton, Donna. *Looking for Little Egypt.* Bloomington, Ind.: IDD Books, 1994.

Cowan, Jane K. *Dance and the Body Politic in Northern Greece.* Princeton, N.J.: Princeton University Press, 1990.

Friedlander, Ira. *The Whirling Dervishes: Being an Account of the Sufi Order, Known as the Mevlevis, and its Founder, the Poet and Mystic, Mevlana Jalalu'ddin Rumi.* London: Wildwood House, 1975.

Graham-Brown, Sarah. *Images of Women: The Portrayal of Women in Photography of the Middle East, 1860–1950.* Reprint of 1988 ed. New York: Columbia University Press, 1992.

Ingber, Judith Brin. *Shorashim: The Roots of Israeli Folkdance.* Dance Perspectives #59, Autumn 1974.

Lawler, Lillian B. *The Dance in Ancient Greece.* Middletown, Conn.: Wesleyan University Press, 1964; reprinted Iowa City: University of Iowa Press, 1974.

Lonsdale, Steven. *Dance and Ritual Play in Greek Religion.* Baltimore: Johns Hopkins University Press, 1993.

Machol Ha'am: The Dance of the Jewish People. Fred Berk, compiler, Susan Reimer, ed. New York: American Zionist Youth Foundation, 1978.

Mishkin, Julie Russo, and Marta Schill. *The Complete Belly Dancer.* Garden City, N.Y.: Doubleday, 1973.

Lane, Edward William. *An Account of the Manners and Customs of the Modern Egyptians.* New York: Dover, 1973.

Lexova, Irena. *Ancient Egyptian Dances, with Drawings Made From the Reproductions of Ancient Egyptian Originals.* Prague, Czechoslovakia: Oriental Institute, 1935. Reprint Brooklyn, New York: Dance Horizons, 1974.

Mourat, Elizabeth Artemis. *The Illusive Veil.* Silver Springs, Md.: Elizabeth Artemis Mourat, 1995.

Richards, Tazz, ed. *The Belly Dance Book: Rediscovering the Oldest Dance.* Concord, Calif.: Backbeat Press, 2000.

Saleh, Magda. *A Documentation of the Ethnic Dance Traditions of the Arab Republic of Egypt.* Ph.D. diss, New York University, 1979. (see also accompanying video documentary *Egypt Dances)*

Shay, Anthony. *Choreophobia: Solo Improvised Dance in the Iranian World.* Costa Mesa, Calif.: Mazda Publishing, 1999.

Van Nieuwkerk, Karin. *A Trade Like Any Other: Female Singers and Dancers in Egypt.* Austin, Tex.: University of Texas Press, 1995.

Nonprint resources

Artemis Dances!, prod. Elizabeth Artemis Mourat, ed. Yasmin, 47 min, Serpentine Communications, Inc., 1998. Videocassette.

The Dancer's Toolkit Vol. 1: Building the Foundation, prod. Baraka, 78 min.. Videocassette.

Dances of Egypt, prod. Aisha Ali, 60 min., Presented by Associated Research in Arab Folklore (ARAF), 1991. Videocassette.

Egypt Dances, conceived by Magda Saleh, dir. Ibrahim El Moky, prod. Egyptian Cinema Organization International Productions, 90 min., 1977. Videocassette. (See also Saleh's accompanying dissertation *A Documentation of the Ethnic Dance Traditions of the Arab Republic of Egypt.)*

Folk Dances of Egypt and the Sudan, dir. Morocco, prod. Middle Eastern Television Productions, 60 min., 1984. Videocassette.

Marrakech Folk Festival, dir. Morocco, prod. Middle Eastern Television Productions, 58 min.. Videocassette.
The Stars of Egypt, prod. Hossam Ramzy and Aischa, 513 min., Ramzy Music International, Ltd. and Trade, 1994. Videocassette.
Stars of Egyptian Dance I and II, dir. Morocco, prod. Middle Eastern Television Productions, 77 min. and 75 min., 1984. Videocassettes.

OCEANIA

This section contains sources on Oceanic dance traditions. Areas include: Australia, Bellona, Fiji, Melanesia, Micronesia, New Zealand, Papua New Guinea, Philippines, Poynesia, Rapanui, Samoa, Tahiti, and Tonga. For specific background information, see the *International Encyclopedia of Dance,* which contains an overview article, "Oceanic Dance Traditions," and related articles on Australian Aboriginal Dance, and individual countries. See also the sections on Dance Ethnology and the Anthropology of Dance, Sacred and Liturgical Dance, and Asia for related sources.

Print resources
Alejandro, Reynaldo G. *Philippine Dance: Mainstream and Crosscurrents.* Manila: Vera-Reyes, 1978.
Bayanihan. Jose Lardizabal [et al.]. Manila: Bayanihan Folk Arts Center, 1987.
Dances of ASEAN. Zainal Abiddin Tinggal, general ed. Brunei Darussalam: Association of South East Asian Nations, ASEAN Committee on Culture and Information, 1998.
    Chapters on Brunei Darussalam, Indonesia, Malaysia, Philippines, Singapore, and Thailand.
Ginn, Victoria. *The Spirited Earth: Dance, Myth, and Ritual from South Asia to the South Pacific.* New York: Rizzoli, 1990.
    Not an anthropological study; useful instead for the striking photographic images.
Kaeppler, Adrienne L. *Hula Pahu Hawaiian Drum Dances.* Volume 1. *Ha'a and Hula Pahu: Sacred Movements.* Honolulu: Bishop Museum, 1993.
————. *Poetry in Motion: Studies of Tongan Dance.* Tonga: Vava'u Press, 1993.
Malinowski, Bronislaw. *Argonauts of the Western Pacific.* New York: E.P. Dutton and Co., 1922.

McLean, Mervyn. *An Annotated Bibliography of Oceanic Music and Dance*. Auckland: Polynesian Society, 1981. Supplement, 1981.

Moyle, Alice M. *Music and Dance in Traditional Aboriginal Culture*. Melbourne: Monash University Frankston Campus, 1991.

Ness, Sally Ann. *Body, Movement, and Culture: Kinesthetic and Visual Symbolism in a Philippine Community*. Philadelphia: University of Pennsylvania Press, 1992.

Stillman, Amy K. *Sacred Hula: the Historical Hula 'Ala'apapa*. Honolulu: Bishop Museum Press, 1998.

Thomas, Allan. *New Song and Dance from the Central Pacific: Creating and Performing the Fatele of Tokelau in the Islands and in New Zealand*. Stuyvesant, N.Y.: Pendragon Press, 1996. Dance and Music series, no. 9.

Van Zile, Judy. *The Japanese Bon Dance in Hawaii*. Hawaii: Press Pacifica, 1982.

Nonprint resources

The JVC video anthology of World Music and Dance, Vol. 29–30: Oceania I & II. Barre, Vt.: Multicultural Media, 1973–1986. Videocassette.

African American Dance

The African American influence on dance is wide ranging from social and ritual dance styles to concert dance and stage performance. Included in this section are general overviews on the influences of African Americans on dance in the United States through recent phenomena such as breakdancing and hip-hop. For additional works, consult the sections on Dance Biographies and Autobiographies, Africa, the Americas, Dance Ethnology and the Anthrolpology of Dance, Variety Dance, Jazz Dance, Tap Dance, Modern and Postmodern Dance, Ballet, Dance Theory, and European and American Social Dance, as well as the Latin American Dance, African Caribbean Dance, and the Africa and Americas sections.

Print resources

Adamczyk, Alice J. *Black Dance: An Annotated Bibliography*. Garland Reference Library of the Humanities; vol. 558. New York: Garland, 1989.

Afro-American Anthropology: ContemporaryPerspectives. Edited by
    Norman E. Whitten and John F. Szwed. NewYork: Collier &
    McMillan, Ltd., 1970.
        See Roger Abrahams' and John F. Szwed's essays for
        examples.
Aschenbrenner, Joyce. *Katherine Dunham: Reflections on the Social and
    Political Contexts of Afro-American Dance.* New York: CORD
    Inc., 1981.
Banes, Sally. *Writing Dancing in the Age of Postmodernism.*
    Middletown, Conn.: Wesleyan University Press; Hanover:
    University Press of New England, 1994.
        See Chapter III entitled "The African American Connec-
        tion" for a discussion of breakdancing.
Droppin' Science: Critical Essays on Rap Music and Hip-Hop Culture.
    Edited by William Eric Perkins. Philadelphia, Penn.: Temple
    University Press, 1996.
Emery, Lynne Fauley. *Black Dance: From 1619 to Today.* 2nd.
    rev. ed. Pennington , N.J.: Princeton Book Co., 1988.
Fresh, Mr. *Breakdancing.* New York: Avon Books, 1984.
Goler, Veta Diane. *Dancing Herself: Choreography, Autobiography,
    and the Expression of the Black Woman Self in the Work of
    Dianne McIntyre, Blondell Cummings, and Jawole Willa Jo
    Zollar.* Ph.D. Dissertation, Emory University, 1994.
Gottschild, Brenda Dixon. *Digging the Africanist Presence in American
    Performance: Dance and Other Contexts.* Westport, Conn.: Green-
    wood Press, 1996.
———. *Waltzing in the Dark : African American Vaudeville and Race
    Politics in the Swing Era.* 1st ed. New York: St. Martin's Press, 2000.
Haskins, James. *Black Dance in America: A History Through Its People.*
    New York: Thomas Y. Cromwell, 1990.
Hazzard-Gordon, Katrina. *Jookin': The Rise of Social Dance Forma-
    tions in African-American Culture.* Philadelphia: Temple Univer-
    sity Press, 1990.
Kebede, Ashenafi. *Roots of Black Music: The Vocal, Instrumental and
    Dance Heritage of Africa and Black America.* Trenton, N.J.: Africa
    World Press, 1995.
Long, Richard A. *The Black Tradition in American Dance*, with
    photographs selected and annotated by Joe Nash. New York:
    Rizzoli, 1989; Smithmark, 1995.

Malone, Jacqui. *Steppin' on the Blues: The Visible Rhythms of African American Dance.* Urbana: University of Illinois Press, 1996.

Mapp, Edward. *Directory of Blacks in the Performing Arts.* 2nd Ed. Metuchen, N.J.: Scarecrow Press, 1990.

Roberts, John W. *From Hucklebuck to Hip-Hop: Social Dancing in the African American Community in Philadelphia.* Philadelphia: ODUNDE, Inc., 1995.

Rose, Tricia. *Black Noise: Rap Music and Black Culture in Contemporary America.* Hanover, N.H.: Wesleyan University Press. Published by University Press of New England, 1994.

Stearns, Marshall Winslow and Jean Stearns. *Jazz Dance: The Story of American Vernacular Dance.* New York: Schirmer Books, 1979; rev. ed., Da Capo Press, 1994.

Thorpe, Edward. *Black Dance.* Woodstock, N.Y.: Overlook Press, 1990.

White, Shane, and Graham White. *Stylin': African American Expressive Culture From Its Beginnings to the Zoot Suit.* Ithaca, N.Y.: Cornell University Press, 1998.

Nonprint resources

Dance Black America. Producers, D.A. Pennebaker and Chris Hegedus. 87 min. Pennington, N.J. : Dance Horizons Video, 1984. Videocassette.

Electric Boogie. Directed by Freke Vuijst and produced by Tana Ross, 30 minutes, New York: Filmakers Library, 1983. Videocassette.

That's Black Entertainment: African–American Contributions in Film and Music 1903–1944. 106 min., distr., North Hollywood, California: OnDeck Home Entertainment, 1997. Videocassette.

The Spirit Moves: A Jazz Documentary, prod. Mura Dehn, *Part 1: Jazz Dance 1900–1950,* 45 min., *Part 2: Savoy Ballroom of Harlem 1950s,* 30 min. *Part 3: Postwar Era,* 40 min., distr. Tango Catalog, Btt. TV. Videocassette.

African Caribbean

The works in this section represent dances from the Caribbean nations. The dance discussed has origins in ritual, folk, social dancing and exhibition dancing. Several general works trace the origins and influences of African Caribbean dance. Much of the contemporary literatures are in the form of ethnographic studies. See also the sections on Dance Ethnology and the Anthropology of Dance, African American Dance, Latin American Dance, Jazz Dance, European and American Social Dance, Modern and Postmodern Dance, and Dance Theory, as well as the Africa section.

Print resources

Afro-American Anthropology: ContemporaryPerspectives. Edited by Norman E. Whitten and John F. Szwed, NewYork: Collier & McMillan, Ltd., 1970.

  See Roger Abrahams' and John F. Szwed's essays for examples.

Ahye, Molly. *Cradle of Caribbean Dance: Beryl McBurnie and the Little Carib Theatre.* Petit Valley, Trinidad and Tobago: Heritage Cultures, 1983.

———. *Golden Heritage: The Dance in Trinidad and Tobago.* Petit Valley, Trinidad and Tobago: Heritage Cultures, 1978.

Blackness in L.A. and the Caribbean: Social Dynamics and Cultural Transformation. Edited by Norman E. Whittier, Jr. and Arlene Torres. Bloomingtin, Ind.: Indiana University Press, 1998.

Boggs, Vernon. *Salsiology: Afro Cuban Music and the Evolution of Salsa in New York City.* New York: Greenwood Press, 1992.

Browning, Barbara. *Samba: Resistance in Motion.* Bloomington, Ind.: Indiana University Press, 1995.

Carty, Hilary S. *Folk Dances of Jamaica: an Insight; A Study of Five Folk Dances of Jamaica with Regard to the Origins, History, Development, Contemporary Setting and Dance Technique of Each.* London: Dance Books; Pennington, N.J.: Distributed in U.S. by Princeton Book Company, 1988.

Courlander, Harold, "Dance and Dance Drama in Haiti" in Boas, Franziska, ed. *The Function of Dance in Human Society.* Republication of the 1944 edition. Brooklyn, N.Y.: Dance Horizons, 1972.

Cowley, John. *Carnival, Canbouley and Calypso: Traditions in the Making.* Cambridge: Cambridge University Press, 1996.

Daniel, Yvonne. *Rumba: Dance and Social Change in Contemporary Cuba.* Bloomington: Indiana University Press, 1995.

Delgado, Celeste Fraser, and Jose Esteban Munoz, ed. *Everynight Life: Culture and Dance in Latin America.* Durham: Duke University Press, 1997.

Deren, Maya. *A Documentary Biography and Collected Works*. Veve Clark, ed. New York: Anthology Film Archives/Film Culture, 1984.

    Working process of a pioneer artist in cinedance and in the Haitian rituals of voudoun.

Dunham, Katherine. *Dances of Haiti*. Los Angeles: Center for Afro-American Studies, University of California, 1983.

———. *Island Possessed*. Chicago: University of Chicago Press, 1994.

Emery, Lynne Fauley. *Black Dance: From 1619 to Today*. 2nd rev. ed. Pennington , N.J.: Princeton Book Co. , 1988.

Fleurant, Gerdes. *Dancing Spirits: Rhythms and Rituals of Haitian Vodun, the Rada Rite*. Westport, Conn..: Greenwood Press, 1996.

Leaf, Earl. *Isles of Rhythm*. New York: A.S. Barnes, 1948.

Lekis, Lisa. *Folk Dances of Latin America*. New York: Scarecrow Press, 1958.

———. *"The Origin and Development of Ethnic Caribbean Dance and Music."* Ph.D. diss., University of Florida, 1956.

Nettleford, Rex M. *Dance Jamaica : Cultural Definition and Artistic Discovery: The National Dance Theatre Company of Jamaica, 1962–1983*. New York : Grove Press, 1985.

Nunley, John W., and Judith Bettelheim. *Caribbean Festival Arts: Each and Every Bit of Difference*. Saint Louis: Saint Louis Art Museum; [Seattle]: University of Washington Press, 1988.

Ortiz, Fernando. *Los Bailes y el Teatro de los Negros en el Folklore de Cuba*. La Habana, Cuba, Editorial Letras Cubanas,1993.

Savigliano, Marta. *Tango and the Political Economy of Passion*. Boulder, Colo.: Westview Press, 1995.

Simpson, George E. *The Shango Cult in Trinidad*. Rio Piedras, Institute of Caribbean Studies, University of Puerto Rico, 1965.

Thompson, Donald, and Anne F. Thompson. *Music and Dance in Puerto Rico from the Age of Columbus to Modern Times: An Annotated Bibliography*. Series: Studies in Latin American Music, no. 1. Metuchen, N.J.: Scarecrow Press, 1991.

Vega Drouet, Hector. *Historical and Ethnological Survey on Probable African Origins of the Puerto Rican Bomba*. Ph.D. diss., Wesleyan University, 1979.

Nonprint resources

Divine Horsemen: The Living Gods of Haiti. Directed by Maya Deren. 52 minutes. New York: Mystic Fire Video, 1985. Videocassette.

The JVC/Smithsonian Folkways Video Anthology of Music and Dance of the Americas Volume 4. The Carribbean. Montpelier, Vt. : Distributed by Multicultural Media, 1995. Videocassette.

The JVC Video Anthology of World Music and Dance the Americas II Mexico/Cuba/Bolivia/Argentina / ; Volume 28. Tokyo : JVC, Victor Company of Japan Rounder Records, 1990. Videocassette.

Roots of Rhythm. New York : New Video Group, 1997 [1989]. Videocassette.

Latin American Dance

The following works are representative of dance in Latin America with a focus on popular or urban dance styles, including tango, samba, salsa, and *danzón*. See also the sections on the Americas, African American Dance, Spanish Dance, and Dance Theory for related sources.

Print resources

Azzi, Maria Susana. *Antropologia del Tango: Los Protagonistas.* Buenos Aires: Ediciones de Olavarria, 1991.

Browning, Barbara. *Samba : Resistance in Motion.* Bloomington, Ind.: Indiana University Press, 1995.

Buenosaires, Oscar de. *Tango: A Bibliography: Books, History, People, Words.* Series: A Book's Fingerprints; 7. Albuquerque, N.M.: Fog Publications, 1991.

Coba Andrade, Carlos Alberto G. *Danzas y Bailes en el Ecuador.* Quito, Ecuador: Ediciones Abya-Yala, 1985.

Collier, Simon and Artemis Cooper, Maria Susana Azzi and Richard Martin. *Tango!: The Dance, the Song, the Story.* Special photography by Ken Haas. New York: Thames and Hudson, 1995.

Dallal, Alberto. *La Danza en Mexico en el Siglo XX.* Mexico, D.F.: Consejo Nacional para la Cultura y las Artes, 1994.

Delgado, Celeste Fraser, and Jose Esteban Munoz, ed. *Everynight Life: Culture and Dance in Latin America.* Durham, N.C.: Duke University Press, 1997.

Flores y Escalante, Jesús. *Imágenes del Danzón: Iconografía del Danzón en México.* México, DF: Asociación Mexicana de Estudios Fonográficos, 1994.

Guillermoprieto, Alma. *Samba*. New York: Knopf : Distributed by
Random House, 1990.

La Historia del Tango. 19 volumes. Buenos Aires: Corregidor, 1976–
1987.

Jara Gámez, Simón, Aurelio Rodríguez Yeyo, and Antonio Zedillo
Castillo. *De Cuba con Amor—: el Danzón en México*. México:
Grupo Azabache: Consejo Nacional para la Cultura y las Artes,
Culturas Populares, 1994.

Labraña, Luis. *Tango, una Historia*. Buenos Aires: Ediciones
Corregidor, 1992.

Lekis, Lisa. *Folk Dances of Latin America*. New York: Scarecrow Press,
1958.

Lewis, John Lowell. *Ring of Liberation: Deceptive Discourse in Brazilian Capoeira*. Chicago: University of Chicago Press, 1992.

Londono, Alberto. *Danzas Colombianas*. 2nd ed. Medellín, Colombia: Editorial Universidad de Antioquia, 1988.

Ocampo López, Javier. *El Folclor y los Bailes Típicos Colombianos*.
Manizales, Colombia: Biblioteca de Escritores Calenses, 1981.

Pickenhayn, Jorge Oscar. *Estudio Sobre el Tango*. Buenos Aires:
Editorial Plus Ultra, 1999.

Ramos Smith, Maya. *La Danza en Mexico Durante la Epoca Colonial*.
La Habana: Casa de las Americas, 1979.

———. *El Ballet en México en el Siglo XIX: de la Independencia al Segundo
Imperio (1825–1867)*. México D.F.: Alianza/CNCA, 1991.

———. *Teatro Musical y Danza en el Mexico de la Belle Epoque, 1867–
1910*. Mexico, D.F.: Universidad Autonoma Metropolitana:
Grupo Editorial Gaceta, 1995.

Sareli, Jorge. *El Tango a Través del Tiempo*. México: Editorial Diana,
1992.

Savigliano, Marta. *Tango and the Political Economy of Passion*. Boulder,
Colo.: Westview Press, 1995.

Sevilla, Amparo. *Danza, Cultura y Clases Sociales*. México, DF: INBA,
1990.

Ulloa, Alejandro. *La Salsa en Cali*. Cali, Colombia: Ediciones
Universidad del Valle, 1992.

Vianna, Hermano. *The Mystery of Samba : Popular Music and National
Identity in Brazil*. Edited and translated by John Charles
Chasteen. Chapel Hill, N.C.: University of North Carolina
Press, 1999.

Nonprint resources

The JVC Video Anthology of World Music and Dance. Directors,
Nakagawa Kunihiko, Ichihashi Yuji. *The Americas II*, Volume 28.
Tokyo: JVC, Victor Company of Japan ; Cambridge, MA :
distributed by Rounder Records, 1990. Videocassette.

Tango, Our Dance/ Tango, Baile Nuestro. Produced by Facets Multimedia, Inc. and Chicago Latino Cinema. 70 minutes. Chicago:
Facets Video, 1998. Videorecassette.

Spanish Dance

The following works represent Spanish dance from the 17th and 18th
centuries to the present and the dance of flamenco which originated
in Spain. *The Diccionario Enciclopedico Ilustrado del Flamenco* is a
major work and a useful reference source. Donn Pohren's *The Art of
the Flamenco,* now in it's fifth edition, is recommended. Matteo's *The
Language of Spanish Dance* is a dictionary of useful terms and concepts. The films of Carlos Saura are recommended for the visual
images of flamenco. See also the sections on Latin American Dance,
AfricanCaribbean Dance, Ballet, Modern and Postmodern Dance,
Jazz Dance, European and American Social Dance Traditions,
Dance Ethnology and the Anthropology of Dance, Dance Theory,
and the section on Central and South America.

Print resources

Blas Vega, Jose, and Manuel Rios Ruiz. *Diccionario Enciclopedico
Ilustrado del Flamenco*. 2nd ed. Madrid: Editorial Cinterco,
1990.

Brooks, Lynn Matluck. *The Dances of the Processions of Seville in
Spain's Golden Age*. Series: Teatro del Siglo de Oro. Estudios de
literatura; 4 Kassel: Ed. Reichenberger, 1988.

Dolmetsch, Mabel. *Dances of Spain and Italy from 1400 to 1600.*New
York: Da Capo Press, 1975.

Esses, Maurice. *Dance and Instrumental Diferencias in Spain During
the 17th and Early 18th Centuries*. 3 volumes. Dance and Music
Series, no. 2. Stuyvesant, N.Y.: Pendragon Press, 1992–
c.1994.

> Volume 1. History and Background, Music and Dance
> Volume 2. Musical Transcriptions
> Volume 3. Notes in Spanish and Other Languages

Hughes, Russell Meriwether [La Meri, pseud.] *Spanish Dancing.* New York, A. S. Barnes, 1948.

Ivanova, Anna. *The Dance in Spain.* New York: Praeger Publishers, 1970.

Lewis, Daniel, ed. *Dance in Hispanic Cultures.* Yverdon, Switzerland: Harwood Academic Publishers, 1994.

Matteo (Vittucii, Matteo Marcellus), with Carola Goya. *The Language of Spanish Dance.* Norman: University of Oklahoma Press, 1993.

Pohren, Donn E. *The Art of Flamenco.* 5th ed. Madrid, Spain: Society of Spanish Studies; Westport, Conn.: USA distributor, the Bold Strummer Ltd., 1990.

Salinas Rodriguez, Jose Luis. *Jazz, flamenco, tango: Las orillas de un ancho rio /* Jose Luis Salinas Rodriguez; con un prologo de Horacio Ferrer. Edition: 1a ed. Series: Coleccion/Ensayo (Editorial Catriel) Madrid : Editorial Catriel, 1994.

Schreiner, Claus, ed. Mollie C. Peters, trans. *Flamenco : Gypsy Dance and Music from Andalusia.* Portland, Ore.: Amadeus Press, 1990.

Suarez-Pajares, Javier and Xoan M. Carreira, editors. *The Origins of the Bolero School.* Translated by Elizabeth Coonrod Martinez, Aurelio de la Vega, Lynn Garafola ; English version edited by Lynn Garafola. Series: Studies in dance history ; v. 4, no. 1. Pennington, N.J.: Society of Dance History Scholars, 1993.

Nonprint resources

Flamenco. Directed by Carlos Saura. 100 minutes, New York: New Yorker Video, 1998. Videocassette.

The JVC Video Anthology of World Music and Dance. Europe, Volume 20. Directed by Nakagawa Kunihiko and Ichihashi Yuji.. Tokyo: JVC, Victor Company of Japan ; Cambridge, Mass.: distributed by Rounder Records, 1990. Videocassette.

Sevillanas. Directed by Carlos Saura. 55 minutes. Los Angeles, Calif.: Meridian Video Corporation, 1996. Videocassette.

Sacred and Liturgical Dance

The use of dance for spiritual and religious purposes has been a continuous thread in human history. For specific background information, see the overview article, "Ritual and Dance;" in the *International Encyclopedia of Dance*; the *Encyclopedia's* synoptic outline of contents lists many additional articles including "Asian Dance Traditions—Religious, Philosophical, and Environmental Influence," "Bible, Dance in the," "Christianity and Dance," "Guild Dances," "Liturgical Dance," "Matachines," "Moresca," "Trance Dance," and "Vodun." The resources below are supplemented by listings in the Geographical Traditions section. See also the sections on African American Dance, African Caribbean Dance, Dance Ethnology and the Anthropology of Dance, Dance Theory, and Somatic Studies.

Print resources

Adams, Doug, and Diane Apostolos-Cappadona, editors. *Dance as Religious Studies.* New York: Crossroad Pub. Co., 1990.

Amoss, Pamela. *Coast Salish Spirit Dancing: The Survival of an Ancestral Religion.* Seattle: Univ. of Washington Press, 1978.

Averbuch, Irit. *The Gods Came Dancing: A Study of the Japanese Ritual Dance of Yamabushi Kagura.* Cornell East Asia Series. Ithaca, N.Y.: East Asia Program, Cornell University, 1995.

Bandem, I Made, and Fredrik Eugene De Boer. *Balinese Dance in Transition: Kaja and Kelod.* 2nd ed. Kuala Lumper, New York: Oxford University Press, 1995.

Belo, Jane. *Bali : Rangda and Barong.* Seattle: University of Washington Press, 1966, 1949.

Boddy, Janice Patricia. *Wombs and Alien Spirits: Women, Men and the Zar Cult in Northern Sudan.* Madison, Wis.: University of Wisconsin Press, 1989.

Davies, J.G. *Liturgical Dance: An Historical, Theological, and Practical Handbook.* London: SCM. 1984.

Fleurant, Gerdes. *Dancing Spirits: Rhythms and Rituals of Haitian Vodun, the Rada Rite.* Westport, Conn.: Greenwood Press, 1996.

Ginn, Victoria. *The Spirited Earth: Dance, Myth, and Ritual from South Asia to the South Pacific.* Forward by Keri Hulme. New York: Rizzoli, 1990.

Huet, Michel. *The Dance, Art, and Ritual of Africa.* Text by Jean-Louis Paudrat. Introduction by Jean Laude. New York: Pantheon Books, 1978.

Huhm, Halla Pai. *Kut: Korean Shamanist Rituals.* New Jersey and Seoul: Hollym International Corporation, 1980.

Jones, Evan John. *Sacred Mask, Sacred Dance.* St. Paul, Minn: Llewellyn Publications, 1997.

Korean Shamanism: Revivals, Survivals, and Change. Howard Keith, ed. Korea: Royal Asiatic Society, Korea Branch, 1998.

Rust, E. Gardner. *The Music and Dance of the World's Religions: A Comprehensive, Annotated Bibliography of Materials in the English Language.* Music Reference Collection, No. 54. Westport, Conn.: Greenwood Press, 1996.

Sacred Dance Guild. *Resources in Sacred Dance: Annotated Bibliography from Christian and Jewish Traditions.* Kay Troxell, ed. Rev. ed. Peterborough, N.H.: Sacred Dance Guild, 1991.

Stillman, Amy K. *Sacred Hula: The Historical Hula ala Apapa.* Honolulu: Bishop Museum Press, 1998.

Nonprint resources

Bedhaya: The Sacred Dance, prod. and dir. Shanty Harmayn, 20 min., distr. Stanford University, 1994. Videocassette.

A documentary of three generations of ritual dancers from the court of Surakarta, Indonesia.

Chindo Sikkim Kut, prod. Asia Society, 115 min. distr. Asia Society, New York, 1994. Videocassette.

Shamanistic ceremony performed at Asia Society by the Chindo Sikkim Kut Preservation Group.

Dream Dances of the Kashia Pomo: The Bole-Maru Religious Women's Dances, prod. University of California, Dept. of Anthropology, 30 min., distr. University of California Extension Center, 1964. Videocasette.

Recording of dances of the Pomo people of Central California.

Kontakion: A Song of Praise, chor. Barry Moreland, prod. Thames Television, 26 min., distr. The Media Guild, 1972. Videocassette.

London Contemporary Dance Theatre performs Moreland's contemporary dance depiction of Christ's birth, ministry, crucifixion and resurrection.

Lord of the Dance, Destroyer of Illusion, prod. Franz-Christoph Gierke, dir. Richard Kohn, 108 min., distr. Mystic Fire Video, 1996. Videocassette.

Ritual dances at a religious festival photographed at the Thubten Choling and Chiwong monasteries in Nepal.

Western European Renaissance and Baroque Dance
Works in this section deal with Western European dance of the
fifteenth through eighteenth centuries, dance frequently called
Renaissance and Baroque. Many works have the distinction of
presenting the earliest known efforts to write down, or notate,
western European dance. For summary discussions notation systems,
see Ann Hutchinson Guest's *Choreo-Graphics: A Comparison of Dance
Notation Systems from the Fifteenth Century to the Present*. For anti-
dance works, and sources on the forms and their cultures, see the
extensive bibliography in Joseph Marks's *The Mathers on Dancing*.
Primary sources in this section are included, as they are available in
modern edition, in English translation, or in facsimile, often with
modern commentary. Some works are represented by multiple
editions, not with the intent of providing a comprehensive publication history, but to offer choices during the acquisitions process.
Given the geographic area in which Renaissance and Baroque dance
developed, foreign-language works are cited as well as those in
English. See also the sections on Dance Biographies and Autobiographies, Ballet, Dance Notation ,and Dance Theory.

Print resources
Arbeau, Thoinot. *Orchesographie*. Lengres: Jehan des preyz, 1589,
    1596. Facsimile reprints: Bibliotheca musica Bononiensis, Sez. 2,
    102, Bologna: Forni Editore, 1969; Genève: Slatkine Reprints,
    1970; Genève: Minkoff Reprints, 1972; Hildesheim; New York:
    Georg Olms Publishers, 1980. Trans. by Cyril W. Beaumont as
    Orchesography. London: author, 1925. Beaumont's trans. re-
    printed, Brooklyn, N.Y.: Dance Horizons, 1968. Trans. by Mary
    Stewart Evans as *Orchesography*. New York: Kamin Dance
    Publishers, 1948. Evans's trans. rev. and ed. by Julia Sutton,
    representative steps and dances in Labanotation by Mireille
    Backer. New York: Dover Publications, Inc., 1967.
Barnett, Dene. *The Art of Gesture: The Practices and Principles of
    Eighteenth Century Acting*. With the assistance of Jeanette
    Massy-Westrop. Heidelberg: Carl Winter Universitatsverlag,
    1987.
Baskervill, Charles Read. *The Elizabethan Jig*. 1929, rep. New York:
    Dover Publications, 1965.
Beaujoyeulx, Baltasar de. *Le Balet Comique*. 1582. Facsimile reprint

with intro. by Margaret M. McGowan. Medieval and Renaissance Texts and Studies, 6. Binghamton, N.Y.: Center for Medieval & Early Renaissance Studies, 1982.

Brainard, Ingrid. *The Art of Courtly Dancing in the Early Renaissance. Part II: The Practice of Courtly Dancing.* West Newton, Mass.: I. G. Brainard, 1981

Caroso, Fabritio. *Il ballarino.* Venice, 1581. Facsimile reprint, Monuments of Music and Music Literature (MMMLF), 2nd ser., Music Literature (ML), 46, New York: Broude Brothers, 1967.

————. *Nobiltà di dame.* Venice, 1600. Facsimile reprint, Bibliotheca musica Bononiensis, Sez. 2, 103, Bologna: Forni Editore, 1970. English translation by Julia Sutton, Oxford; New York: Oxford University Press, 1986; rev., corrected and expanded republication as *Courtly Dance of the Renaissance: A New Translation and Edition of the Nobiltà di Dame (1600),* New York: Dover Publications, Inc., 1995.

Compasso, Lutio. *Ballo della gagliarda.* Florence, 1560. Facsimile reprint as *Ballo della gagliarda: Faksimile der Ausgabe von 1560* with English intro. by Barbara Sparti, Freiburg: "fa-gisis" Musik- und Tanzedition, 1995.

Cornazano, Antonio. *Libro dell'arte del danzare.* 1455. Trans. Madeleine Inglehearn and Peggy Forsyth as *The Book on the Art of Dancing*; intro. and notes by Madeleine Inglehearn. London: Dance Books Ltd., 1981.

Crane, Frederick. *Materials for the Study of the Fifteenth Century Basse Danse.* Studies and Documents, 16. Brooklyn, New York: Institute of Mediaeval Music, 1968.

Cunningham, James P. *Dancing in the Inns of Court.* London: Jordan and Sons, 1965.

Davies, Sir John. *Orchestra or, A Poem of Dancing.* E. M. W. Tillyard, ed. London: Chatto & Windus, 1945. Reprints: Dance Horizon Series 24, [Brooklyn], New York: Dance Horizons, 1970; New York: Scholarly Press, 1979.

Feuillet, Raoul-Auger. *Chorégraphie, ou l'art de décrire la dance.* Paris, 1700. Facsimile reprint published with *Recueil de dances, composées par M. Feuillet* and *Recüeil de dances, composées par M. Pecour*, MMMLF, 2nd ser., ML, 130, New York: Broude Brothers, 1968. Facsimile reprint, Hildesheim: George Olms, 1979. 2nd ed. augmented with 4 tables of supplementary steps. Paris: auteur,

Michel Brunet, 1701. Facsimile reprint, Bibliotheca musica Bononiensis, Sez. 2, 105, Bologna: Arnaldo Forni, 1969. *Chorégraphie* trans. by John Weaver as *Orchesography or the Art of Dancing*. London, 1706. Facsimile reprint, Westmead, England: Gregg International, 1971.

Feuillet, Raoul Auger. *Recueil de contredances*. Paris: Feuillet, 1706. Facsimile reprint, MMMLF, 2nd ser., ML, 135, New York: Broude Bros., 1968. Trans. by John Essex as *For the Further Improvement of Dancing,* London: I. Walsh & P. Randall, J. Hare, 1710. Facsimile reprints: Westmead, England: Gregg International, 1970; New York: Dance Horizons, 1970.

Fletcher, Ifan K., Selma Jeanne Cohen, and Roger Londsdale. *Famed for Dance: Essays on the Theory and Practice of Theatrical Dancing in England, 1660-1740*. New York: New York Public Library, 1960. Reprint, New York: Books for Libraries, 1980.

Gallini, Giovanni Andrea. *A Treatise on the Art of Dancing,* London: author, 1762. Facsimile reprint, MMMLF, 2nd ser., ML, 48, New York: Broude Bros., 1967.

Guglielmo Ebreo of Pesaro. *De Pratica Seu Arte Tripudii: On the Practice or Art of Dancing*. Trans. of the 1463 manuscript. Ed., trans. and introduced by Barbara Sparti. Poems trans. by Michael Sullivan. Oxford; New York: Clarendon Press, 1993.

Harris-Warrick, Rebecca and Carol G. Marsh. *Musical Theatre at the Court of Louis XIV: Le Mariage de la Grosse Cathos.* Cambridge; New York: Cambridge University Press, 1994.

Hilton, Wendy. *Dance of Court and Theater: Selected Writings of Wendy Hilton*. Labanotation by Mireille Backer. Stuyvesant, N.Y.: Pendragon Press, 1997.

Hoop, Loes de, and Freek Pliester, comp. *Handlist of the Dance Collection.* Den Haag: Haags Gemeentemuseum, 1982. Issued with *Dance Collection: From the Music Library of the Haags Gemeentemuseum on Microfiche*. Ed. Dick van den Hul. Zug, Switzerland: Inter-Documentation Co.

Howard, Siles. *The Politics of Courtly Dancing in Early Modern England*. Amherst: Univ. of Mass. Press, 1998.

Instruction pour dancer: An anonymous manuscript [ca. 1610]. Edited and introduced by Angene Feves, Ann Lizbeth Langston, Uwe

Schlottermüller, and Eugenia Roucher. Freiburg: "fa-gisis" Musik- und Tanzedition, 2000.

Jenyns, Soame. *The Art of Dancing, a Poem in Three Cantos*. London: J. Robert, 1729. Reprint ed. by Anne Cottis, London: Dance Books; Princeton, N.J.: Princeton Book Company, 1978.

Keller, Kate Van Winkle and Genevieve Shimer. *The Playford Ball: 103 Early English Country Dances, 1651-1820 as Interpreted by Cecil Sharp and His Followers*. Northampton, Mass: The Country Dance and Song Society, 1994.

Kennedy, Judith. *Popular Dances of the Renaissance: a Dance Lesson with Written and Vocal Instructions*. [Ashland, Ore.]: Judith Kennedy, 1985. Audiocassette with instruction booklet.

Kinkeldey, Otto. *A Jewish Dancing Master of the Renaissance: Guglielmo Ebreo*. Dance Horizons Series, 8. Brooklyn, N.Y.: Dance Horizons, 1966.

L'Abbe, Anthony. *A New Collection of Dances*. Intro. by Carol C. Marsh. Music for London Entertainment Series D, Pantomime, Ballet & Social Dance, 2. London: Stainer & Bell, 1991.

Lambranzi, Gregorio. *Neue und curieuse theatralische tantz-schul deliciae theatrales*. Nurnberg: Johann Jacob Wolrab, 1716. Facsimile reprints: with German commentary by Kurt Petermann, English trans. by Michael Talbot, Leipzig: Peters, 1975; with intro. and notes by F. Derra de Moroda, New York: Dance Horizons, 1972. English trans. by F. Derra de Moroda as *New and Curious School of Theatrical Dancing*. Ed. with preface by Cyril W. Beaumont. London: Imperial Society of Teachers of Dancing, 1928. Reprint, New York: Dance Horizons, 1966.

Lauze, F. de. *Apologie de la Danse*. 1623. Facsimile reprint, Genève, Minkoff Reprint, 1977. English trans. by Joan Wildeblood. London: Frederick Muller Ltd., 1952.

Lehner, Marcus. *Manual of Sixteenth-Century Italian Dance Steps*. Freiburg: "fa-gisis" Musik- und Tanzedition, 1997.

Little, Meredith Ellis and Marsh, Carol G. *La Danse Noble: An Inventory of Dances and Sources*. Williamstown, Mass., New York, Nabburg: Broude Brothers Limited, 1992.

Magri, Gennaro. *Trattato teorico-prattico di ballo*. Napoli: Vincenzi Orsino, 1779. Trans. by Mary Skeaping with Anna Ivanova and Irmgard Berry as *Theoretical and Practical Treatise on Dancing*. Ed. I. Berry and Annalisa Fox. London: Dance Books, 1988.

Marks, Joseph. *The Mathers on Dancing.* Brooklyn, N.Y.: Dance Horizons, c. 1975.

Mather, Betty Bang. *Dance Rhythms of the French Baroque: A Handbook for Performance.* With the assistance of Dean M. Karns. Bloomington: Indiana University Press, 1987.

McGowan, Margaret M. *L'art du ballet de cour en France, 1581–1643.* Paris: Editions du Centre Nationale de la Recherche Scientifique, 1963.

Moreau de St.-Méry, Médéric Louis Elie. *Danse. Article extrait d'un ouvrage de M. L. E. Moreau de St.-Méry. Ayant pour titre Répertoire des notions coloniales. Par ordre alphabétique.* Philadelphie: l'auteur, 1796. English trans. with intro. by Lily and Baird Hastings as *Dance: an article drawn from the work by M. L. E. Moreau de St.-Méry entitled: Repertory of colonial information, compiled alphabetically (1796).* Brooklyn, N.Y.: Dance Horizons, 1975.

Negri, Cesare. *Le gratie d'amore.* Milan, 1602. Facsimile reprints: MMMLF, 2nd ser., ML, 141, New York: Broude Brothers, 1969; Bibliotheca musica Bononiensis, Sez. 2, 104, Bologna: Forni, 1969.

Noverre, Jean Georges. *Lettres sur la danse et sur les ballets.* Stutgard [sic]: Aimé Delaroche, 1760. Facsimile reprint, MMMLF, 2nd ser., ML, 47, New York: Broude Bros., 1967. Eng. trans. of selections with commentary by Beaumont as *Letters on Dancing and Ballets.* London: C. W. Beaumont, 1930. 2nd ed. with revised intro. London: C. W. Beaumont, 1951. Reprint, Brooklyn, N.Y.: Dance Horizons, 1966.

Pasch, Johann Georg. *Anleitung sich bei grossen Herrn Höfen und andern beliebt zu machen.* Edited and introduced by Uwe Schlottermüller. In German, with abstracts in English and French; steps translated by Barbara Ravelhofer and Véronique Daniels. Freiburg: "fa-gisis" Musik- und Tanzedition, 2000.

Playford, John. *The English Dancing Master.* London, 1651. Facsimile reprint ed. by Hugh Mellor and Leslie Bridgewater, London: H. Mellor, 1933. Reprint from the 1933 edition, Brooklyn, N.Y.: Dance Horizons, [1976?]. Facsimile reprint with intro., bibliography and notes by Margaret Dean-Smith, London: Schott & Company, Ltd., 1957. Dance Horizons

Pugliese, Patri J. and Joseph Casazza. *Practise for Dauncinge Some Almans & a Pavan, England 1570-1650: A Manual for Instruction.* Cambridge, Mass.: authors, 1980.

Rameau, Pierre. *Abbrégé de la nouvelle Méthode dans l'Art d'Écrire ou
de Tracer toutes sortes de Danses de Ville*.... Paris: auteur, 1725.
Facsimile reprint, Westmead, England: Gregg International,
1972.

Le maître à danser.... Paris: Jean Villette, 1725. Facsimile reprint,
MMMLF, 2nd ser., ML, 45, New York: Broude Brothers, 1967.
Trans. by Cyril W. Beaumont with G. Bickham's plates from
1731 ed. as *The Dancing Master*. London: Beaumont, 1931.
Reprint Brooklyn, N.Y.: Dance Horizons, 1970.

Schwartz, Judith L. and Christena L. Schlundt. *French Court Dance
and Dance Music: A Guide to Primary Source Writings, 1643-1789*.
Dance and Music Series, no. 1. Stuyvesant, N.Y.: Pendragon
Press, 1987.

Smith, A. William, annot. and trans. *Fifteenth-century Dance and
Music: Twelve Transcribed Italian Treatises and Collections in the
Tradition of Domenico da Piacenza*. 2 vols. Dance and Music
Series, no. 4. Stuyvesant, N.Y.: Pendragon Press, 1995.

Thomas, Bernard and Jane Gingell. *The Renaissance Dance Book:
Dances from the Sixteenth and Early Seventeenth Centuries*. London: Pro Musica Edition, 1987. Dance instructions, scores and
parts, audiocassette.

Tomlinson, Kellom. *The Art of Dancing*.... London: author, 1735. *Six
Dances*.... London, 1720. Facsimile reprints, bound together,
England: Gregg International Publishers, 1970; Brooklyn, N.Y.:
Dance Horizons, 1970.

————. *A Work Book by Kellom Tomlinson: Commonplace Book of an
Eighteenth-Century English Dancing Master: a Facsimile Edition*.
Jennifer Shennan, ed. Dance and Music, 6. Stuyvesant, N.Y.:
Pendragon Press, 1992.

Weaver, John. *The Life and Works of John Weaver: An Account of His
Life, Writings and Theatrical Productions with an Annotated
[facsimile] Reprint of His Complete Publications*. Annotations,
intro. by Richard Ralph. Brooklyn, N.Y.: Dance Horizons,
1985.

Winter, Marian Hannah. *The Pre-Romantic Ballet*. London: Pitman
Publishing, 1974. Brooklyn, N.Y.: Dance Horizons, 1975.

Nonprint resources
Il Ballarino: The Art of Renaissance Dance. Produced, and narrated by

Julia Sutton; directed by Julia Sutton and Johannes Holub. Pennington, N.J.: Dance Horizons, Princeton Book Co., 1991. Videocassette.

Baroque Dance, 1675–1725. Conceived by Shirley Wynne and Allegra Fuller Snyder. Produced by Masters and Masterworks Productions, Inc. Directed by Allegra Fuller Snyder. Dist. by Berkeley: University of California Extension Media Center, 1977. Film, Videocassette.

Le gratie d'amore. Produced by Filmocentro, Taller de Danzas Antiguas, Charles Garth and Elizabeth Aldrich. Performed by Taller de Danzas Antiguas and The Court Dance Company of New York. New York: Historical Dance Foundation, 1992. Videocassette.

Introduction to Baroque Dance–Dance Types. Vols. 1 and 2. Paige Whitley Baugess and Thomas Baird. New Bern, N.C.: Down East Dance, 1999. Videocassette.

Ballet

In Europe and America, ballet is synonymous with classical dance and is widely recognized as one of the oldest and most familiar forms of dance. As the field of dance has increasingly embraced a more global perspective, classical dance is not only synonomous with ballet forms, and has different meanings within other cultures. Moreover, ballet is a term that has been applied to works in modern dance as well. This section primarily represents Pan-European and American ballet traditions, and includes works on ballet as a form and tradition not only within Europe and America, but also within other countries such as China. See also the sections under Dance Styles, Forms, and Traditions, the sections on Biographies and Autobiographies, Dance Notation, Criticism, Choreography, Dance Theory, Dance and Related Arts, Dance Education, and Dance in Commercial Theater and Movies for related sources.

Print resources

Amberg, George. *Ballet in America: The Emergence of an American Art.* New York: Da Capo Press, 1983.

American Ballet Theatre: A Twenty-five Year Retrospective. Kansas City, Mo.: Andrews McMeel Publishing, 1999.

Anawalt, Sasha. *The Joffrey Ballet: Robert Joffrey and the Making of an American Dance Company*. New York: Scribner, 1996.

Anderson, Jack. *The One and Only: The Ballet Russe de Monte Carlo*. Pennington, N.J.: Princeton Book Co., 1995.

Barringer, Janice and Sarah Schlesinger. *The Pointe Book: Shoes, Training and Technique*, rev. ed. Pennington, N.J.: Princeton Book Co., 1999.

Beaumont, Cyril W. *The Ballet called Giselle*. Princeton N.J.: Princeton Book Co., 1988.

———. *The Ballet called Swan Lake*. New York: Dance Horizons, 1982.

———. *Michel Fokine & His Ballets*. Pennington, N.J.: Princeton Book Co., 1997.

Bland, Alexander. *The Royal Ballet: The First Fifty Years*. Garden City, N.Y.: Doubleday, 1981.

Blasis, Carlo *An Elementary Treatise upon the Theory and Practice of the Art of Dancing*. Translated by Mary Stewart Evans. New York: Dover Publications, 1968.

A Century of Russian Ballet: Documents and Accounts, 1810–1910. Selected and translated by Roland John Wiley. New York: Oxford University Press, 1990.

Chazin-Bennahum, Judith. *Dance in the Shadow of the Gillotine*. Carbondale: Southern Illinois University Press, 1988.

———. *The Ballets of Antony Tudor: Studies in Psyche and Satire*. New York: Oxford University Press, 1994.

Choreography by George Balanchine: A Catalogue of Works. New York: Viking, 1984.

Clarke, Mary. *Ballet: An Ilustrated History*. New York: Universe Books, 1978.

Cohen, Selma Jeanne. *Next Week, Swan Lake: Reflections on Dance and Dances*. Middletown, Conn.: Wesleyan University Press, 1982.

Dunning, Jennifer. *"But first a school": The First Fifty Years of the School of American Ballet*. New York: Viking, 1985.

Flindt, Vivi, and Knud A. Jurgensen. *Bournonville Ballet Technique: Fifty Enchainments*. London: Dance Books, 1992.
    A videotape of the same title is also available.

Garafola, Lynn. *Diaghilev's Ballets Russes*. New York: Oxford University Press, 1989.

Nonprint resources

American Ballet Theatre in San Francisco, prod. National Video
Corporation, dir. Brian Lage, 105 minutes, distr. Dance Horizons, Corinth, 1985. Videocassette.
> Contains excerpts of Tudor's *Lilac Garden,* Taylor's *Airs,* and
> Taylor-Corbett's *Great Galloping Gottschalk.*

American Ballet Theatre Now, prod. WNET/Dance in America. 83
minutes, distr. PBS, 1998. Videocassette.
> Contains excerpts from *The Leaves Are Fading, Cruel World,
> Romeo and Juliet, Black Swan* pas de deux, and *Don Quixote*
> pas de deux.

Anna Karenina, chor. Maya Plisetskaya, mus. Rodion Shchedrin,
prod. B. Boguslavsky and B. Geller, dir. Margarita Philihina, 81
minutes, Corinth Films, distr. Kultur, 1974, 1988. Videocassette.

Antony Tudor, prod. Mans Reutersward, dir. Viola Aberle and
Gerd Andersson, , 57 minutes, for NOS Television and
Sveriges Television, distr. Dance Horizons Video, 1985.
Videocassettte.

*The Balanchine Celebration: The Four Temperaments, Divertimento #15
and Tzigane,* prod. Emile Ardolino, dir. Merrill Brockway, 60
minutes, 1977, distr. Nonesuch, Dance Horizons. Videocassette.
> Originally released as *Choreography by Balanchine, Part 1* and
> broadcast on Dance in America.

The Balanchine Celebration: Prodigal Son and Chaconne, prod. Emile
Ardolino and Judy Kinberg, dir. Merrill Brockway, 60 minutes,
1978, distr. Nonesuch, Dance Horizons. Videocassette.
> Originally released as *Choreography by Balanchine, Part 3* and
> broadcast on Dance in America.

The Balanchine Essays: Arabesque. 45 minutes, 1995; *Passé and Attitude.* 43 minutes, 1996; *Port de Bras and Epaulement.* 45 minutes,
1996, prod. George Balanchine Foundation and Tatge/Lasseur,
dir. Merrill Brockway, distr. Nonesuch, Dance Horizons,
WarnerVision, Viewfinders. Videocassettes.

The Ballerinas, prod. Joseph Wishy, dir. Beppe Menegatti and Tzio
Tani, 108 minutes, 1985, distr. Kultur, Dance Horizons, Home
Vision. Videocassette.
> Carla Fracci in romantic and classical repertory, with part-
> ners Peter Schaufuss, Vladimir Vasiliev, Richard Cragun and
> Charles Jude.

Baryshnikov at Wolftrap. 50 minutes, 1976, distr. Kultur, Dance
  Horizons, Viewfinders, Home Vision. Videocassette.
      With Gelsey Kirkland and American Ballet Theatre in *Don
  Quixote* pas de deux, *Spectre de la Rose.*
Baryshnikov Dances Sinatra., chor: Twyla Tharp, prod. Don Mischer,
  dir. Don Mischer and Twyla Tharp, 60 minutes, 1995, distr.
  Dance Horizons, Viewfinders, Home Vision. Videocassette.
      With American Ballet Theatre in *Sinatra Suite* and *Push
  Comes to Shove.*
Basic Principles of Partnering, prod. and dir. Patricia Dickenson, 47
  minutes, 1994, distr. Dance Horizons. Videocassette.
La Bayadere, prod. Fiona Morris and Paul Kafno, dir. Derek Bailey,
  120 minutes, 1991, distr. Kultur, Home Vision, Viewfinders,
  Dance Horizons. Videocassette.
      Britain's Royal Ballet led by Altynai Asylmuratova, Irek
  Mukhamedov and Darcey Bussell.
Billboards: The Joffrey's Rock Ballet, chor. Laura Dean, Charles
  Moulton, Peter Pucci, and Margo Sappington, mus. Prince, prod.
  NYC Arts and WNET/New York, dir. Gerald Arpino and
  Derek Bailey, 56 minutes, distr. Dance Horizons Video, 1993.
  Videocassette.
Bournonville Ballet Technique: Fifty Enchainments, prod. Jakob
  Mydtskov, dir. Vivi Flindt, 38 minutes, distr. Dance Horizons
  Video, 1992. Videocassette.
The Children of Theatre Street, prod. Patricia Barnes, 92 minutes.,
  distr. Dance Horizons Video, 1978. Videocassette.
      About the training of young dancers at the Vaganova School
  attached to the Kirov Ballet in St. Petersburg.
Cinderella, chor. Rudolf Nureyev, prod. La Sept and BBC, dir. Colin
  Nears, 125 minutes, distrs. Corinth, Dance Horizons Video,
  Viewfinders, 1987. Videocassette.
      With Sylvie Guillem and the Paris Opera Ballet in a revi-
  sionist version of the fairytale.
Creole Giselle, chor. Frederic Franklin after Coralli, Perrot, and Petipa,
  prod. Dance Theatre of Harlem and Danmarks Radio, dir.
  Thomas Grimm, 88 minutes, distrs. Kultur, Home Vision,
  Facets, Dance Horizons Video, 1987. Videocassette.
      Dance Theatre of Harlem, with Virginia Johnson and Eddie
  Shellman.

Dance Theatre of Harlem, prod. Emile Ardolino, dir. Merrill
   Brockway, 60 minutes, distr. Indiana University, 1977. Videocas-
   sette.
   Documentary on the company with performace excerpts of
   repertory by Louis Johnson, Geoffrey Holder, George
   Balanchine, and Lester Horton.
Dancing for Mr. B.: Six Balanchine Ballerinas, prod. and dir. Anne
   Belle, 90 minutes, distr. Direct Cinema, WarnerVision,
   Viewfinders, Dance Horizons, Facets, 1989. Videocassette.
   Interviews and dance sequences with Mary Ellen Moylan,
   Maria Tallchief, Melissa Hayden, Allegra Kent, Merrill
   Ashley, and Darci Kistler.
An Evening with Jiri Kylian and the Netherlands Dance Theater,
   (alternate title *Four by Kylian*), chor. Jiri Kylian, prod. RM Arts,
   dir. Hans Hulscher and Torbjorn Ehrnvall, 38 minutes, distrs.
   Home Vision, Dance Horizons Video, Viewfinders, Corinth,
   1987. Videocassette.
   Contains *Svadebka (Les Noces), La Cathedrale Engloutie,
   Sinfonietta*, and *Torso*.
An Evening with the Royal Ballet, prod. and dir. Anthony Havelock-
   Allen, 87 minutes, distr. Kultur, Dance Horizons, Viewfinders,
   Home Vision, 1985.
   Starring Rudolf Nureyev and Margot Fonteyn in *La Corsaire*
   pas de deux and *Les Sylphides*, and Frederick Ashton's *La
   Valse*.
Gaité Parisienne, chor. Léonide Massine, dir. Victor Jessen, 38
   minutes, distr. Dance Horizons, Viewfinders, Corinth, 1954.
   Videocassette.
   Danced by Alexandra Davilova, Frederic Franklin, Leon
   Danielian and the Ballet Russe de Monte Carlo.
Giselle, prod. E. Grigorian, dir. V. Grave, 90 minutes, distr. Kultur,
   Corinth, Viewfinders, Facets, 1979. Videocassette.
   Bolshoi Ballet performance with Natalia Bessmertnova and
   Leonide Lavrovsky.
Nutcracker, chor. Mikhail Baryshnikov, prod. Herman Krawitz, 85
   minutes, distr. MGM/UA, Home Vision, Viewfinders, Corinth,
   1977. Videocassette.
   Gelsey Kirkland and Mikhail Baryshnikov with American
   Ballet Theatre.

Nutcracker, chor. George Balanchine, prod. Robert Krasnow and
Robert Hurwitz, dir. Emile Ardolino, 90 minutes, distr. Warner
Home Video, 1993. Videocassette.
  Darci Kistler, Damian Woetzel, Kyra Nichols and New York
  City Ballet with Macaulay Culkin.
On the Move: Central Ballet of China, prod. Sidney and Mary Yung
Kantor and Catherine Tatge, dir. Merrill Brockway, 60 min.,
distr. Direct Line Cinema, 1987. Videocassette.
Onegin, chor. John Cranko, prod. National Video Corporation, dir.
Norman Campbell and Reid Anderson, 96 minutes, distr. Home
Vision, ViewFinders, Corinth, 1987. Videocassette.
  Sabine Allemann and Frank Augustyn, with the National
  Ballet of Canada.
Pointe by Pointe, prod. Ross Alley, dir. Gred Lofton, 45 minutes, distr.
Kultur, Dance Horizons, Home Vision, 1988. Videocassette.
  Teacher Barbara Fewster presents technique for working in
  the pointe shoes of classical ballet.
The Red Shoes, chor. Robert Helpmann and Léonide Massine, prod. J.
Arthur Rank Organization, dir. Michael Powell, 135 minutes,
distr. Films Inc., Paramount, Home Vision, Corinth, 1948.
Videocassette.
  Famous fiction film in which a ballerina must choose
  between art and love, starring Moira Shearer, Robert
  Helpmann and Léonide Massine.
Road to the Stamping Ground, chor. Jiri Kylian, mus. Carlos Chavez,
prod. RM Arts, NOS-TV Holland, and Polygram Picgtures, dir.
David Muir and Hans Hulscher, 60 minutes, distrs. Home
Vision, Dance Horizons, Viewfinders, 1984. Videocassette.
  Kylians's experiences with Australian aboriginal dances and the
  resulting theatrical work performed by Nederlands Dans Theater.
Robert Schuman's "Davidsbundlertanze", chor. George Balanchine,
prod. Catheine Tatge, dir. Merrill Brockway, 86 minutes, distr.
Corinth, WarnerVision, Viewfinders, Dancer Horizons, Facets,
1981. Videocassette.
  New York City Ballet with Karin von Aroldingen, Ib
  Andersen, Adam Luders and Suzanne Farrell.
Romeo and Juliet, chor. Angelin Preljocaj, prod. La Sept and RM
Arts, dir. Alexandre Tarta, 90 minutes, distr. Home Vision,
Corinth, Facets, 1993. Videocassette.

Nontraditional version of the story danced by the Lyon
Opera Ballet with Pascale Doye and Nicolas Ducloux.

Romeo and Juliet, chor. Kenneth MacMillan, prod. Royal Academy
Productions, dir. Paul Czinner, 124 minutes, distr. Kultur, Home
Vision, Dance Horizons, Viewfinders, Facets, 1966. Videocas-
sette.

Margot Fonteyn and Rudolf Nureyev, with England's Royal
Ballet.

Romeo and Juliet, chor. Leonid Lavrovsky, dir. L. Arnstam, 95 minutes, distr. Corinth, Kultur, Home Vision, Viewfinders, 1954.
Videocassette.

Galina Ulanova and Yuri Zhdanov with the Bolshoi Ballet.

Choreography by Balanchine, Part 2, prod. WNET/13 Dance in
America, dir. Merrill Brockway, 90 minutes, distr. WNET Video
Distribution, 1977. Videocassette.

A slightly shortened version of *Jewels*, danced by New York
City Ballet with Merrill Ashley, Patricia McBride, Suzanne
Farrell and Peter Martins.

Swan Lake, prod. National Video Corporation, dir. John Michael
Phillips, 137 minutes, distr. Viewfinders, 1986. Videocassette.

Natalia Makarova and Anthony Dowell with England's
Royal Ballet.

Sylvie Guillem at Work, prod. RM Arts and La Sept, dir. André
Labarthe, 53 minutes, distr. Home Vision, Viewfinders, Corinth,
1988. Videocassette.

The Turning Point, prod. Twentieth Century Fox, dir. Herbert Ross,
119 minutes, distr. Films Inc., CBS/Fox, Corinth, 1977. Videocassette.

A fiction film set in a ballet company, starring Mikhail
Baryshnikov, Leslie Browne, and Alexandra Danilova.

Video Dictionary of Classical Ballet, dir. Robert Beck, 270 minutes,
distr. Kultur, Dance Horizons, Viewfinders, Home Vision, 1983.
Videocassette.

The classical vocabulary is demonstrated in real-time and
slow motion sequences by dancers Georgina Parkinson,
Denise Jackson, Merrill Ashley, and Kevin McKenzie.

White Nights, chor. Twyla Tharp, Gregory Hines, and Roland Petit,
prod. Columbia Pictures, dir. Taylor Hackford, 135 minutes,
distr. Films Inc, Corinth, Columbia Tristar, 1985. Videocassette.

Ballet star Mikhail Baryshnikov and tap star Gregory Hines in a fiction film based in St. Petersburg with scenes in the Kirov Theater.

Modern and Postmodern Dance

Until the last decade, a bibliography like this would have recommended only books that describe modern and postmodern dance. Now, thanks to videocassettes, CD Roms and other new media, it is possible to build a library of the dances themselves. Albums of photographs and other primary resources remain as essential sources of dance documentation, but videorecordings have become alternative texts for analytic and stylistic information. Included in this section are videotapes, which summarize the pioneer artists and the central works of modern dance. For newer artists there are many gaps. As dance videotapes and other media enter the mainstream marketplace, more dances by living artists are expected to become available for library purchase. Also included in this section are selected books of criticism, as they define the field and provide acute verbal descriptions of particular dances. See also the sections on Dance Biographies and Autobiographies, Geographical Traditions, African American Dance, Choreography, Dance Notation, and Dance Theory.

Print resources

Alvin Ailey American Dance Theater: Jack Mitchell Photographs.
    Foreward by Judith Jamison; introduction by Richard Philp.
    Kansas City, Mo.: Andrews and McMeel, 1993.
Anderson, Jack. *Art Without Boundaries: The World of Modern Dance.*
    Iowa City: University of Iowa Press, 1997.
Art Performs Life: Merce Cunningham, Meredith Monk, Bill T. Jones.
    Minneapolis: Walker Art Center, 1998.
        An illlustrated exhibition catalog with essays by Sally Banes,
        Philippe Vergne, Siri Engberg, Kellie Jones and Philip
        Blither.
Banes, Sally. *Subversive Expectations: Performance Art and Paratheater
    in New York. 1976–85.* Ann Arbor, Mich.: University of Michigan Press, 1998.
    ———. *Writing Dancing in the Age of Postmodernism.* Hanover, N.H.:
Wesleyan University Press, 1994.

————.*Democracy's Body: Judson Dance Theater 1962–1964.* Durham, N.C.: Duke University Press, 1993.

————. *Greenwich Village 1963: Avant-Garde Performance and the Effervescent Body.* Durham, N.C.: Duke University Press, 1993.

————. *Terpsichore in Sneakers: Post-Modern Dance.* Hanover, N.H.: University Press of New England, 1987.

The Black Tradition in American Modern Dance. Durham, N.C.: American Dance Festival, 1988.

Brazil, Tom. *Dances by Mark Morris* New York: Dance Research Foundation, 1993.

Brown, Jean Morrison, Naomi Mindlin, and Charles H. Woodford, eds. *The Vision of Modern Dance in the Words of Its Creators.* Hightstown, N.J.: Princeton Book Company, 1998.

Burt, Ramsay. *Alien Bodies: Representations of Modernity, "Race," and Nation in Early Modern Dance.* New York: Routledge, 1998.

Butoh: Dance of the Dark Soul. Photographs by Ethan Hoffman, commentaries by Mark Holborn, Yukio Mishima and Tatsumi Hijikata. New York: Aperture, 1987.

Cohen, Selma Jeanne, ed. *Modern Dance: Seven Statements of Belief.* Hanover, N.H.: Wesleyan University Press, University Press of New England, 1965.

José Limón, Anna Sokolow, Paul Taylor, and Donald McKayle are among the seven choreographers.

Daly, Ann. *Done into Dance: Isadora Duncan in America.* Bloomington: Indiana University Press, 1995.

Duncan, Dorée, Carol Pratl, and Cynthia Splatt, eds. *Life into Art: Isadora Duncan and Her World,* foreward by Agnes De Mille. New York: W.W. Norton, 1993. Extensively illustrated.

Fraleigh, Sandra. *Dancing into Darkness: Butoh, Zen, and Japan.* Pittsburgh: University of Pittsburgh Press, 1999.

Garafola, Lynn , ed., *Of, By and For the People: Dancing on the Left in the 1930s.* Studies in Dance History, v. 5, no. 1, spring 1994. Distr. University Press of New England.

Graff, Ellen. *Stepping Left: Dance and Politics in New York City, 1928–1942.* Durham, N.C.: Duke University Press, 1997.

Greenfield, Lois. *Airborne: The New Dance Photography of Lois Greenfield.* With texts by William A. Ewing and Daniel Girardin. San Francisco: Chronicle Books, 1998.

Helpern, Alice. *The Technique of Martha Graham*. Studies in Dance History, vol. 2, no. 2, 1991. Society of Dance History Scholars.

Horst, Louis and Carroll Russell. *Modern Dance Forms, in Relation to Other Modern Arts*. New York: Dance Observer, 1937; reprint, with an introduction by Janet Mansfield Soares, Hightstown, N.J.: Princeton Book Company, 1987.

> The new edition of the book has an accompanying audiocassette *Music for Modern Dance Forms*, narrated by Janet Soares, pianist Elisenda Fabrégas, distr. Princeton Book Company.

Jackson, Naomi. *Converging Movements: Modern Dance and Jewish Culture at the 92nd Street Y*. Hanover, N.H.: University Press of New England, 2000.

Jordan, Stephanie. *Striding Out: Aspects of Contemporary and New Dance in Britain*. London: Dance Books, 1992.

Jowitt, Deborah, ed. *Meredith Monk*. Baltimore: Johns Hopkins University Press, 1997.

Kendall, Elizabeth. *Where She Danced: The Birth of American Art-Dance*. New York: Knopf, 1979; Berkeley: Univ. of California Press, 1979; Berkeley: University of California Press, 1984.

Kreemer, Connie, ed. *Further Steps Fifteen Choreographers on Modern Dance*, New York: Harper & Row, 1987.

> Statements by artists including Louis Falco, Molissa Fenley, Bill T. Jones and Arne Zane, Nancy Meehan, Gail Conrad, and Kei Takei.

Kriegsman, Sali Ann. *Modern Dance in America—The Bennington Years*. Boston: G.K. Hall/Macmillan, 1981.

Livet, Anne, ed.*Contemporary Dance: An Anthology of Lectures, Interviews and Essays*, New York: Abbeville Press, 1978. Extensively illustrated.

Lloyd, Margaret. *The Borzoi Book of Modern Dance*. New York: Alfred A. Knopf, 1949; NY: Dance Horizons, 1969, 1974.

Long, Richard A. *The Black Tradition in American Dance*, with photographs selected and annotated by Joe Nash. New York: Rizzoli, 1989; Smithmark, 1995.

Manning, Susan. *Ecstasy and the Demon: Feminism and Nationalism in the Dances of Mary Wigman*. Berkeley: University of California Press, 1993.

Martin, John Joseph. *The Modern Dance*. New York: A.S. Barnes, 1933; Princeton, N.J.: Princeton Book Co., 1989.

> Re-publication of a series of lectures describing the major figures of 1930s American modern dance.

McDonagh, Don. *The Complete Guide to Modern Dance*. Garden City, N.Y.: Doubleday, 1976.

———. *The Rise and Fall and Rise of Modern Dance*. New York: Outerbridge and Dienstfrey, 1970; Pennington, N.J.: A Capella, 1990.

Morgan, Barbara. *Martha Graham, Sixteen Dances in Photographs*. Dobbs Ferry, New York: Morgan & Morgan, 1990.

Perces, Marjorie with Ana Marie Forsythe and Cheryl Bell. *The Dance Technique of Lester Horton*. Hightstown, N.J.: Princeton Book Company, 1992.

Perron, Wendy ed. *Judson Dance Theater: 1962–1966*. Bennington, Vt.: Bennington College, 1981.

Preston-Dunlop, Valerie ed. *Schrifttanz: German Modern Dance Writings of the 1920s and 1930s*. Princeton Book Company.

> Includes writings of Rudolf Laban, Mary Wigman, and Oskar Schlemmer.

Rainer, Yvonne. *Work 1961–73*. Halifax, N.S.: Press of the Nova Scotia College of Art and Design; New York: New York University Press, 1974.

Ruyter, Nancy Lee Chalfa. *Reformers and Visionaries: The Americanization of the Art of Dance*. New York: Dance Horizons, 1979.

Shawn, Ted. *Every Little Movement: A Book about Francois Delsarte, the Man and His Philosophy, His Science and Applied Aesthetics, the Application of this Science to the Art of Dance, the Influence of Delsarte on American Dance*. Brooklyn: Dance Horizons, 1963, rev. 1968

Siegel, Marcia B. *The Shapes of Change: Images of Modern Dance*. Boston: Houghton-Mifflin, 1979; Berkeley: University of California Press, 1985.

Tracy, Robert, ed. *Goddess: Martha Graham's Dancers Remember*. New York: Limelight Editions, 1997.

Trager, Philip and Ralph Lemon. *Persephone*. Hanover, N.H.: Wesleyan University Press/University Press of New England, 1996.

> A collaboration in choreography by Ralph Lemon and photography by Philip Trager.

Vaughan, David. *Merce Cunningham: Fifty Years*. New York: Aperture, 1997.

Nonprint resources

Acrobats of God, chor. Martha Graham, mus. Carlos Surinach, decor.

Isamu Noguchi, prod. John Houseman, 22 min., distr. Pyramid
Film & Video, 1970. Videocassette.

Alvin Ailey: Memories and Visions, dir. Stan Lathan, 54 min., WNET/
Thirteen, distr. Phoenix/BFA Films, 1974. Videocassette.

>Ailey discusses his work, with performance excerpts includ-
ing *Mary Lou's Mass* and *Lark Ascending*.

Ailey Dances, prod. James Lipton, dir. Tim Kiley, 90 min., Kultur
Video, 1982. Videocassette.

>Alvin Ailey American Dance Theater performs *Night
Creature, Cry, Lark Ascending*, and *Revelations*.

Anna Sokolow: Choreographer, 20 min., Princeton Visual Communications, distr. Princeton Book Co., Facets Video, 1978. Videocassette.

>Sokolow discusses her work, illustrated by rehearsal and
performance footage of *Rooms*.

Beach Birds for Camera, chor. Merce Cunningham, dir. Elliot Caplan,
28 min., Cunningham Dance Foundation, 1993. Videocassette.

Beyond the Mainstream, prod. and dir. Merrill Brockway, 60 min.,
WNET/Thirteen, distr. Films Inc., 1980. Videocassette.

>Influences of happenings, the Judson movement, Grand
Union, and contact improvization on modern dance.

Bill T. Jones: Dancing in the Promised Land, prod. and dir. Mischa Scorer,
59 min., VIEW Video, Facets Video, 1994. Videocassette.

>Documentary on the preparation and performance of *Last
Supper at Uncle Tom's Cabin/The Promised Land*.

Butoh: Body on the Edge of Crisis, prod. and dir. Michael Blackwood,
written by Bonnie Sue Stein, 90 min., Michel Blackwood
Productions, 1990. Videocassette.

The Catherine Wheel, chor. and dir. Twyla Tharp, mus. David Byrne,
decor, Santo Loquasto, prod. Alan Yantob, 87 min., Thorn
EMI/HBO Video, Electra Nonesuch, Facets Video, 1982.
Videocassette.

Changing Steps, chor. Merce Cunningham, dir. Elliot Caplan, mus.
John Cage, 35 min., distr. Cunningham Dance Foundation,
1989. Videocassette.

Clytemnestra, chor. Martha Graham, mus. Halim el-Dabh, decor
Isamu Noguchi, 90 min., WNET/Thirteen, distr. Films Inc.
Video, 1979. Videocassette.

Charles Weidman: On His Own, narrated by Alwin Nikolais, prod.
Miriam Cooper, Charles Weidman Dance Foundation, dir.

Virginia Brooks, 60 min., Dance Horizons Video, Facets Video,
1990. Videocassette.

> Contains archival footage and modern reconstructed perfor-
> mances including *Lynchtown*.

Dance Black America, Prod. D.A. Pennebaker and Chris Hegedus,
narrator Geoffrey Holder, 87 min., distr. Princeton Book Co.,
Facets Video, 1984. Videocassette.

> Performance selections from a 4-day festival at Brooklyn
> Academy of Music, includes works by Asadate Dafora,
> Katherine Dunham, Charles Moore. and Eleo Pomare.

Dance: Four Pioneers, prod. Jac Venza for WNET/13, dir. Charles S.
Dubin, distr. Indiana University, University of Minnesota, 30
minutes, 1966. Videocassette.

> The film introduces the modern dance pioneers associ-
> ated with Bennington College in the 1930s: Martha
> Graham, Doris Humphrey, Charles Weidman, and Hanya
> Holm.

*The Dance Works of Doris Humphrey: With My Red Fires and New
Dance*, perf. in 1972 by the American Dance Festival Company,
60 min., Dance Horizons Video, 1989. Videocassette.

Denishawn: The Birth of Modern Dance, prod. Center Dance Collective, 40 min., Kultur Video, Facets Video, 1988. Videocassette.

> Contains archival footage and modern reconstructed perfor-
> mances of the choreography of Ruth St. Denis and Ted
> Shawn.

Digital Dance 2. Interviews with Sioban Davies, Lloyd Newson and
Ian Spink, 1989, distr. National Resource Centre for Dance.

> Three British choreographers talk with critic Stephanie
> Jordan about their work. Videocassette.

Donald McKayle, prod. and dir. Douglas Rosenberg, 60 min., American Dance Festival and University of Wisconsin, Madison, distr.
Dance Horizons Videos. Videocassette.

> Interview with McKayle and performances of *Games,
> Rainbow 'round My Shoulder* and *Distant Drum*.

Doris Humphrey Technique: The Creative Potential, dir. Ernestine
Stodelle, 45 min., Dance Horizons Video, 1992. Videocassette.

> Contains *Air for the G String* and *Two Ecstatic Themes.*

Eiko and Koma/Land, chor. Eiko and Koma, mus. Robert Mirabal,
prod. and dir. Douglas Rosenberg, American Dance Festival and

the University of Wisconsin, Madison, 60 minutes, distr. The
Kitchen, 1994. Videocassette.

Erick Hawkins' America, dir. Sidney J. Palmer, 57 min., South Carolina Educational Television, distr. Dance Horizons Video, Facets
Video, 1988. Videocassette.

    Erick Hawkins Dance Company performs *Plains Daybreak,
Hurrah!*, and *God's Angry Man*.

Ellis Island, chor., mus., and dir. Meredith Monk, prod. and co-dir. Bob
Rosen, 28 min., House Foundation for the Arts, 1991. Videocassette.

European Tanztheater, prod. Isa Partsch-Bergsohn, dir. Hal Bergsohn,
60 min., Dance Horizons Video, 1997. Videocassette.

Falling Down Stairs, chor. Mark Morris, prod. Niv Fichman, dir.
Barbara Willis Sweete, distr. Rhombus International/Sony
Classical Video, 56 min., 1995. Videocassette.

    Records the collaboration of cellist Yo Yo Ma and the Mark
Morris Dance Company in a dance to Bach's *Suite #3 for
Unaccompanied Cello*.

Genius on the Wrong Coast, prod. and dir. Lelia Goldoni, 90 min.,
distr. Green River Road, 1993. Videocassette.

    On the dance-theater of Lester Horton.

Griot New York, chor. Garth Fagan, mus. Wynton Marsalis, 87 min.,
WNET/Thirteen and Sony Classical Film and Video, 1995.
Videocassette.

Hanya: Portrait of a Dance Pioneer, prod. Nancy Mason Hauser and
Marilyn Christofori, dir. John Ittelson, 55 min., distr. Facets
Video, 1984. Videocassette.

    Influential modern dancer who also created for Broadway,
notably *My Fair Lady*.

Hoppla!, chor. Anna Teresa de Keersmaeker, prod. Marie-Pascale
Osterrieth and Hugo de Greef, mus. Bartok, 53 min., distr.
Editions de Voir, 1988. Videocassette.

If you couldn't see me and M.O., chor. Trisha Brown, 70 min., filmed in
performance at the Jacob's Pillow Dance Festival, 1995, distr.
Trisha Brown Dance Company. Videocassette.

Isadora Duncan Dance: Technique and Repertory, dir. Julia Levien and
Andrea Mantell Seidel, 60 min., Dance Horizons Video, 1994/
Videocassette.

Isadora Duncan: Movement from the Soul, prod. and dir. Dayna
Goldfine and Daniel Geller with KQED, 60 min., distr. The

Video Catalog, 1988. Videocassette.

> Documentary on Isadora's life with dance reconstructions by Madeleine Lytton and Lori Belilove.

José Limón Technique with Daniel Lewis, prod. Dennis Diamond, 55 min., distr. Dance Horizons Video, 1987. Videocassette.

Lester Horton Technique: The Warm-Up, dir. Ana Marie Forsythe and Marjorie Perces, 45 min., Dance Horizons Video, 1990. Videocassette.

Martha Graham: An American Original in Performance, prod. and dir. Nathan Kroll, 93 min., distr. Kultur Video, Phoenix/BFA Films, Facets Video. Videocassette.

> Contains *A Dancer's World* (1957), *Night Journey* (1981), and *Appalachian Spring* (1958).

Martha Graham: The Dancer Revealed, prod. Dominique Lasseur, dir. Catherine Tatge, 57 min., distr. Dance Horizons Video, 1994. Videocassette.

> Biographical documentary on Graham.

Mary Wigman: When the Fire Dances Between Two Poles, prod. and dir. Allegra Fuller Snyder, 41 min., Dance Horizons Video, 1990. Videocassette.

> Contains archival footage of Wigman's repertory.

The Men Who Danced: The Story of Ted Shawn's Male Dancers, 1933–1940, 30 min., Dance Horizons Video, 1986. Videocassette.

> Includes archival footage and modern reconstructed performances.

Pilobolus. dir. Emile Ardolino and Judy Kinberg, prod. Merrill Brockway , 60 min., distr. WarnerVision Entertainment, 1977. Videocassette.

Points in Space, chor. Merce Cunningham, mus. John Cage, prod. Bob Lockyer, dir. Elliot Caplan and Merce Cunningham, 55 min., Cunningham Dance Foundation, distr. by Kultur Video, 1986. Videocassette.

Postmodern Dance: Judson and Grand Union, (Eye on Dance, 307), prod. Celia Ipiotis and Jeff Bush, 28 min., ARC Videodance, 1990. Videocassette.

> Yvonne Rainer and Sara Rudner discuss the formation and influences of the Judson movement. Both dancers perform Rainer's *Trio A*.

Quarry, chor. and mus. Meredith Monk, prod. and dir. Amram Nowak, 86 min., House Foundation for the Arts and Dance

Collection of The New York Public Library, distr House Foundation for the Arts, 1978. Videocassette.

Retracing Steps: American Dance Since Postmodernism, prod. Manfred Grater, dir. Michael Blackwood, written by Sally Banes, 88 min., Michael Blackwood Productions, 1988. Videocassette.

   Interviews, rehearsal and performance of artists including Stephen Petronio, Johanna Boyce, Bill T. Jones and Arnie Zane, and Blondell Cummings.

Rosas Danst Rosas, chor. Anna Teresa de Keersmaeker, prod. Sophie Schoukens and Jan Roekens, dir. Thierry de Mey, mus. Thierry de Mey and Peter Vermeersch, presented by Sophimages and Avila, 57 min., distr. Avila, 1996. Videocassette.

Set and Reset, chor. Trisha Brown, mus. Laurie Anderson, decor Robert Rauschenberg, prod. and dir. Susan Dowling, 22 min., WGBH-TV, distr. by Trisha Brown Dance Company, 1985. Videocassette.

Speaking in Tongues, chor. Paul Taylor, decor. Santo Loquasto, prod. Judy Kinberg, dir. Matthew Diamond, 58 min., Thirteen/ WNET and Amaya Distribution, distr. by Facets Video, PBS Video Distribution, 1991. Videocassette.

Toulouse Television Project, chor. Trisha Brown, dir. Jean-Francois Jung, 41 min., F.R. 3 and La Sept, distr. Trisha Brown Dance Company, 1987. Videocassette.

   Contains *Newark, Accumulation with talking* plus *Watermotor*, and *Group Primary Accumulation*.

A Tribute to Alvin Ailey, prod. and dir. Thomas Grimm, 120 min., Danmarks Radio and RM Arts, distr. by Public Media Home Vision/Films Incorporated, 1992. Videocassette.

   Alvin Ailey American Dance Theater performs works including *For Bird with Love* and *Memoria*.

Triple Duo, chor. Douglas Dunn, prod. and dir. Rudolph Burckhardt, mus. Elliott Carter, 16 min., distr. Burckhardt, 1989. Videocassette.

Trisha and Carmen, chor. Trisha Brown, prod. and dir. Burt Barr, 13 min., distr. Electronic Arts Intermix, Museum of Modern Art, 1988. Videocassette.

Tympani, chor. Laura Dean, prod. and dir. Kathryn Esher, 30 min., distr. KCTA-TV, 1981. Videocassette.

Walkaround Time, chor. Merce Cunningham, mus. David Behrman, decor Jasper Johns after Marcel Duchamp, dir. Charles Atlas, 48 min., distr. Cunningham Dance Foundation, 1973. Videocassette.

The Wrecker's Ball: Three Dances by Paul Taylor, prod. and dir. Matthew Diamond, 56 min., Dance in America/WNET, distr. Dance Horizons Video, WNET Video Distribution, 1996. Videocassette.

> Contains *Company B, Funny Papers*, and *A Field of Grass*.

Jazz Dance

Jazz dance is an evolving cross-cultural phenomenon, strongly influenced by African and European traditions, which has grown primarily within American culture. This list includes books and films that deal with the conceptual nature of the jazz dance form; its influential teachers, dancers, and choreographers. Manuals and how-to guides have not been included. As jazz dance and tap dance frequently intermix, also consult the Tap Dance section. As jazz dance is featured in some of Hollywood's greatest movies, also consult the section on Dance in Commercial Theater and Movies. See also the sections on Dance Biographies and Autobiographies, African American Dance, African Caribbean Dance, and Dance Theory.

Print resources

Baral, Robert. *Revue: The Great Broadway Period*. New York: Fleet Press, 1970.

Bordman, Gerald. *The American Musical Theater*. New York: Oxford University Press, 1982.

Boross, Robert. *Image Of Perfection: The Freestyle Dance Of Matt Mattox*. New York: New York University Press, 1994.

Cayou, Dolores. *Modern Jazz Dance*. London: Dance Books. Ltd., 1976.

Croce, Arlene. *The Fred Astaire and Ginger Rogers Book*. New York: Dutton, 1972.

Dodge, Richard Pryor. *Hot Jazz and Jazz Dance*. Pryor Dodge, ed. New York: Oxford University Press, 1995.

Emery, Lynne. Fauley. *Black Dance: From 1619 To Today*. 2nd. rev. ed. Pennington , N.J.: Princeton Book Company, 1988.

Fortunato, Joanne *Major Influences Affecting The Development Of Jazz Dance, 1950-1971*. Marietta, Ga.: Dance Press, 1974.

Giordano, Gus. *Anthology Of American Jazz Dance*. Evanston, Ill.: Orion Publishing House, 1975.

————. *Jazz Dance Class: Beginning thru Advanced*. Pennington, N.J.: Princeton Book Co., 1992.

Gottfried, Martin. *All His Jazz: The Life and Death of Bob Fosse*. New York: Bantam, 1990.

Hazzard-Gordon, Katrina. *Jookin': The Rise Of Social Dance Formations In The African American Culture*. Philadelphia: Temple University Press, 1990.

Hill, Constance Valis. *Brotherhood in Rhythm: The Jazz Tap Dancing of the Nicholas Brothers*. New York: Oxford University Press, 2000.

Hirshorn, Clive. *The Hollywood Musical*. New York: Crown, 1981.

Kimball, Robert and William Bolcom. *Reminiscing with Sissle and Blake*. New York: The Viking Press, 1973.

Kislan, Richard. *Hoofing on Broadway: A History of Show Dancing*. Englewood Cliffs, N.J.: Prentice Hall, 1987.

Kraines, Minda. G. and Esther Kan. *Jump Into Jazz*. Mountain View, Calif.: Mayfield Publishing, 1990.

Kriegel, Lorraine. Person and Kimberly Chandler-Vaccaro. *Jazz Dance Today*. Agoura, Calif.: West Publishing, 1994.

Kriegel, Lorraine Person and Francis James Roach. *Luigi's Jazz Warm Up and Introduction to Jazz Style & Technique*. Pennington, N.J.: Princeton Book Company, 1997.

La Pointe-Crump, Janice and Kim Staley. *Discovering Jazz Dance: America's Energy And Soul*. Dubuque, Iowa.: Brown & Benchmark, 1992.

Loney, Glenn Meredith. *Unsung Genius: The Passion of Dancer-Choreographer Jack Cole*. New York: Franklin Watts Company, 1984.

————, ed. *Musical Theater in America*. Westport, Conn.: Greenwood Press, 1981.

Long, Richard A. *The Black Tradition in American Dance*, with photographs selected and annotated by Joe Nash. New York: Rizzoli, 1989; Smithmark, 1995.

Malone, Jacqui. *Steppin' on the Blues: The Visible Rhythms of African American Dance*. University of Illinois Press, 1996.

Mandelbaum, Ken. *A Chorus Line and the Musicals of Michael Bennett*. New York: St. Martin Press, 1975.

Mates, Julian. *America's Musical Stage: Two Hundred Years of Musical Theater*. Westport, Conn.: Greenwood Press, 1975.

Miller, Norma. *Swingin' At The Savoy: The Memoir Of A Jazz Dancer.* Philadelphia: Temple University Press, 1996.

Sabatine, Jean. *Technique And Styles Of Jazz Dancing.* Waldwick, N.J.: Hoctor Dance Records, 1969.

Sampson, Henry T. *Blacks in Blackface: A Source Book on Early Black Musical Shows.* Metuchen, N.J.: Scarecrow Press, 1980.

Stearns, Marshall Winslow and Jean Stearns. *Jazz Dance: The Story of American Vernacular Dance.* New York: Schirmer Books, 1979; rev. ed., Da Capo Press, 1994.

Traguth, Fred. *Modern Jazz Dance.* Englewood Cliffs, N.J.: Prentice-Hall, 1983.

Thorpe, Edward. *Black Dance.* Woodstock, N.Y.: The Overlook Press, 1990.

Yudkoff, Alvin. *Gene Kelly: A Life of Dance and Dreams.* New York: Watson-Guptil Publications, 2000

Nonprint resources

Call of the Jitterbug, dir. Jesper Sorensen, Vibeke Winding and Tana Ross, 35 min., distr. Filmmakers Library, 1988. Videocassette.

Glances at the Past: Documentation of Jazz Dance, prod. Celia Ipiotis and Jeff Bush, dir. Richard Sheridan, 27 minutes, dist. ARC Video, Eye on Dance #58, 1982. Videocassette.

In a Jazz Way: A Portrait of Mura Dehn. prod. Louise Ghertler and Pamela Katz, 28 min., distr. Filmmakers Library, 1986. Videocassette.

Swinging at the Savoy: Francie Manning's Story, prod. Rosemary Hemp, 23 min., distr. Living Traditions, 1995. Videocassette.

The Spirit Moves: A Jazz Documentary, prod. Mura Dehn, *Part 1: Jazz Dance 1900-1950,* 45 min., *Part 2: Savoy Ballroom of Harlem 1950s,* 30 min. *Part 3: Postwar Era,* 40 min., distr. Tango Catalog, Btt. TV. Videocassette.

Tap Dance

Although tap and jazz instruction are separate in today's dance world, the two dance forms stem from common crosscultural roots. Included in this section are works specifically related to tap, including books and films that deal with the conceptual nature of the tap dance form; its influential teachers, dancers, and choreographers. Manuals and how-to guides have not been included. As tap dance and jazz dance frequently intermix, see also the Jazz dance section; as tap dance is featured in some of Hollywood's greatest movies, consult the section on Dance in Commercial Theater and Movies. See also the sections on Dance Biographies and Autobiographies, African American and African Carribean dance.

Print resources

Cowger, Elizabeth. *The Souls of Your Feet: A Tap Dance Guide for Rhythm Explorers*. Acia Gray and Carol Felaser, photographers. Austin, Tex.: Grand Weaver's Publishing

Feldman, Anita. *Inside Tap: Technique and Improvisation for Today's Tap Dancer*. Pennington, N.J.: Princeton Book Co., 1996.

Frank, Rusty E. *Tap!: The Greatest Tap Dance Stars and Their Stories, 1900–1955*. Rev. ed. New York: Da Capo Press, c.1994.

Glover, Savion and Bruce Weber. *Savion!: My Life in Tap*. New York: W. Morrow, 2000.

Hill, Constance Valis. *Brotherhood in Rhythm: The Jazz Tap Dancing of the Nicholas Brothers*. New York: Oxford University Press, 2000.
> History of jazz tap in America as well as biographies of the Nicholas Brothers.

Kislan, Richard. *Hoofing on Broadway: A History of Show Dancing*. New York: Prentice Hall Press, c. 1987

Knowles, Mark. *The Tap Dance Dictionary*. New York: McFarland and Co., 1997.

Stearns, Marshall Winslow and Jean Stearns. *Jazz Dance: The Story of American Vernacular Dance*. New York: Schirmer Books, 1979; rev. ed., Da Capo Press, 1994.

Nonprint resources

Jazz Hoofer: Baby Laurence, prod. and dir. Bill Hancock, 28 min., distr. Rhapsody Films, 1981. Videocassette.

Masters of Tap, prod. Charles Thompson, dir. Jolyon Wimhurst, 61 min., distr. Home Vision, 1983. Videocassette.

No Maps On My Taps. Produced and directed by George T. Nirenberg. 59 min. Franklin Lakes, N.J.: Direct Cinema Ltd., 1979. Videocassette.

TapDancin', prod. and dir. Christian Blackwood, 58 min., distr. Michael Blackwod Productions, 1980. Videocassette.

European and American Social Dance Traditions
Folk dancing
This section focuses on traditional social dances in Europe, with some representation of Israeli and Latin American traditions. For specific literaure on these cultures, see the section on Latin American dance, and the section on the Mediterranean and the Near-East. Unlike other sections, the nature of the literature on folk dancing makes it essential to include ethnographic studies as well as teaching manuals. See also the section on Dance Ethnography and the Anthropology of Dance. The study and recreational revival of folk dances in the twentieth century also resulted in popularized international social dance groups. Additional information can be acquired from the collections of local folk dance groups. See also the sections on Dance Notation, and Dance Ethnology and the Anthropology of Dance for related sources.

Print resources

Allenby Jaffé, Nigel. *Folk Dance of Europe*. Kirby Malham, Skipton, North Yorkshire, England: Folk Dance Enterprises, 1990.

Barrand, Anthony G. *Six Fools and a Dancer: The Timeless Way of the Morris*. Plainfield, Vt.: Northern Harmony Publishing Company, 1991.

Berruti, P. *Manual de danzas nativas: coreografías, historia y texto poético de las danzas*. Buenos Aires: Editorial Escolar, 1971.

Buckland, Theresa. *Traditional Dance*. Crewe, England: Crewe and Alsagar College of Higher Education, 1982.

Buckman, Peter. *Let's Dance: Social, Ballroom & Folk Dancing*. Picture research by Enid Moore. New York: Paddington Press, 1978.

Casey, Betty. *International Folk Dancing U.S.A*. Garden City, N.Y.: Doubleday, 1981.

Chandler, Keith. *Ribbons, Bells, and Squeaking Fiddles: The Social History of Morris Dancing in the English South Midlands, 1660-1900*. Middlesex, U.K.: Hisarlik Press, 1993.

Corrsin, Stephen D. *Sword Dancing in Europe: A History*. Enfield Lock, U.K.: Hisarlik Press, 1997.

Duggan, Anne Schley, Jeanette Schlottmann, and Abbie Rutledge. *Folk Dances of Scandinavia*. New York, A. S. Barnes and Co., 1948.

Dunin, Elsie Ivancich, comp. and ed. *Dance Research: Published or*

Publicly Presented by Members of the Study Group on Ethnochoreology. Los Angeles: International Council for Traditional Music, Study Group on Ethnochoreology, 1989– .

Dziewanowska, Ada. *Polish Folk Dances and Songs : A Step-By-Step Guide.* New York : Hippocrene Books, 1997.

Eden, Yaakov. *Moving in International Circles.* 2nd ed. Dubuque, Iowa : Kendall/Hunt, 1995.

Flett, J.P. and T.M. *Traditional Dancing in Scotland.* London and Boston: Routledge and Kegan Paul, 1964.

Forrest, John. *The History of Morris Dancing, 1458-1750.* Studies in Early English Drama, 5. Toronto: University of Toronto Press, 1999.

Giurchescu, Anca with Sunni Bloland. *Romanian Traditional Dance: A Contextual and Structural Approach.* Mill Valley, Calif.: Wild Flower Press, 1995.

Greene, Hank, ed. *Square and Folk Dancing: A Complete Guide for Students, Teachers, and Callers.* Illustrations by Manosalvas. New York: Harper and Row, 1984.

Harris, Jane A, Anne M. Pittman, and Marlys S. Waller. *Dance A While: A Handbook for Folk, Square, Contra and Social Dance.* 7th ed. New York: MacMillan, 1995.

Hunt, Yvonne M. *Traditional Dance in Greek Culture.* Athens: Centre for Asia Minor Studies, Music Folklore Archive, 1996.

Katsarova-Kukudova, Raina and Kiril Djenev. *Bulgarian Folk Dances.* Translated by Nevena Geliazkova and Marguerite Alexieva. Cambridge, Mass.: Slavica Publishers; Pittsburgh: in cooperation with Duquesne University Tamburitzans Institute of Folk Arts, 1976.

Lane, Christy and Susan Langhout. *Multicultural Folk Dance Guide.* Champaign, Ill. : Human Kinetics, 1998–. v. 1. Hora (Israel). Hukilau (Hawaii). Savila se bela loza (Serbia).Virginia reel (United States). D'hammerschmiedsgselln (Germany). Highlife (Ghana). Alunelul (Romania). Yanko (China). El jarabe tapatio (Mexico)

Lawson, Joan. *European Folk Dance; Its National and Musical Characteristics.* Illustrations by Iris Brooke. Published under the auspices of the Imperial Society of Teachers of Dancing. London: Pitman, 1962, reprint of the revised edition of 1955.
    Includes music and directions for 73 dances.

Lekis, Lisa. *Folk Dances of Latin America.* New York: Scarecrow, 1958.

Loyola, Margot. *Bailes de tierra en Chile.* 2nd. ed. Valparaíso:
Ediciones Universitarias de Valparaíso, 1980.

Lynch, Larry. *Set Dances of Ireland : Tradition & Evolution.* San
Francisco, Calif.: Seádna, 1991.
Includes step directions and history.

Major, Alice. *Ukrainian Shumka Dancers: Tradition in Motion.*
Edmonton, Canada: Reidmore Books, 1991.

Rodríguez Amado, Gustavo. *Música y Danzas en las Fiestas del Perú.*
Arequipa [Peru]: Universidad Nacional de San Agustín:
Universidad Católica de Santa María, 1995.

Romero, Raúl R., ed. *Música, Danzas y Máscaras en los Andes.* Ana
María Béjar [et al]. Lima : Pontificia Universidad Católica del
Perú: Instituto Riva-Aguero, Proyecto de Preservación de la
Música Tradicional Andina, 1993.

Sharp, Cecil J. and Maud Karpeles. *The Country Dance Book.* London, Novello and Company, 1918. Reprint. East Ardsley, England: EP Publishing, 1976.

Shepherd, Robbie. *Let's Have a Ceilidh: The Essential Guide to Scottish
Dancing.* Edinburgh: Canongate Press, 1992.

Venable, Lucy, and Fred Berk. *Ten Folk Dances in Labanotation.* New
York : M. Witmark, 1959.
Includes music arranged for piano and notation for
Cherkessia, Schottische step, Sarajevka kolo, Seven step,
Korobushka, Masquerade, Road to the isles, Greek dance,
Norwegian polka, and Debka.

Ysursa, John M. *Basque Dance.* Boise, Idaho: Tamarack Books, 1995.

Nonprint resources

Ethnic Dance Around the World. Prod. and distr. BFA Educational
Media, 1983. Videocassette.

Movement Style and Cultures. Part 1, Dance and human history
(1974) . Part 2, Palm play (1977). Part 3, Step style (1977).Writ-
ten, edited, and produced by Alan Lomax for the Choreometrics
Project, Department of Anthropology, Columbia University.
Movement advisor: Irmgard Bartenieff. Dance and movement
analyst: Forrestine Paulay.
Examples of folk and ethnic dance from each continent are
compared cross-culturally to illustrate the relationship of
movement style to social structure.

The JVC Video Anthology of World Music and Dance. Fujii Tomoaki,
   ed.; assistant editors, Omori Yasuhiro, Sakurai Tetsuo; in
   collaboration with the National Museum of Ethnology
   (Osaka).
      Guide issued to accompany *The JVC Video Anthology of World
      Music and Dance,* a set of 30 VHS videocassettes produced by
      Ichikawa Katsumori, directed by Nakagawa Kunihiko.

Square, Old Time, Contra, and Round Dancing
While these forms can be viewed as North American traditions, all
of these styles of dance are currently enjoyed internationally, having
become part of popular culture. Because these are community based
recreations, documentation and research have been scant until recently.
Most work still exists in the form of periodical literature, though a
number of theses and dissertations have been produced within the past
few years. The following section is comprised of academic or scholarly
books which place the dancing in historical, social, or aesthetic context,
and key collections of dances by individuals central to the development
of these dance forms in popular culture in the United States. Some
specific handbooks and directories are included. See also the section on
Dance Notation and Dance Ethnology and the Anthropology of Dance
for related sources.

Print resources
Abrahams, Roger D. *Singing the Master: The Emergence of African
      American Culture in the Plantation South.* New York: Pantheon
      Books, 1992.
         This study elucidates the African American influence in
         American square dance.
California Square Dancer Blue Book. Alhambra, Calif.: Myrick Press,
      1969– .
Casey, Betty. *The Complete Book of Square Dancing (and Round
      Dancing).* Garden City, N.Y.: Doubleday and Co., 1976.
Dalsemer, Robert G. *West Virginia Square Dances.* New York: Coun-
      try Dance and Song Society, 1982.
Damon, S. Foster. *The History of Square Dancing.* Barre, Mass.: Barre
      Gazette, 1957.
Dart, Mary M. *Contra Dance Choreography: A Reflection of Social
      Change.* Portland, Ore.: Garland Publishing, Inc., 1995.

Gunzenhauser, Margot. *The Square Dance and Contra Dance Handbook: Calls, Dance Movements, Music Glossary, Bibliography, Discography and Directories.* Jefferson, N.C.: McFarland, 1996.

Jones, Loyal. *Minstrel of the Appalachians: The Story of Bascom Lamar Lunsford.* Boone, N.C.: Appalachian Consortium Press, 1984.

National Square Dance Directory. Gordon Goss, ed. Jackson, Miss.: NSD Products, 1978– .

Quigley, Colin. *Close to the Floor: Folk Dance in Newfoundland.* St.John's: Memorial University of Newfoundland Folklore and Language Publications, 1985.

Sanella, Ted. *Balance and Swing: A Collection of Fifty-five Squares, Contras, and Triplets in the New England Tradition with Music for Each Dance.* Northampton, Mass.: Country Dance and Song, 1990.

Shaw, Lloyd. *Cowboy Dances: A Collection of Western Square Dances.* Caldwell, Idaho: Caxton Printers, 1950.

Smith, Frank. *The Appalachian Square Dance.* Berea, Ky.: Berea College, 1955.

Sharp, Cecil J. and Maud Karpeles. *The Country Dance Book, Part V: The Running Set.* London: Novello and Company, 1918. Reprint. East Ardsley, England: EP Publishing, 1976.

Spalding, Susan Eike and Jane Harris Woodside. *Communities in Motion: Dance, Tradition, and Community in America's Southeast and Beyond.* Westport, Conn.: Greenwood Press, 1995.

Tolman, Beth and Ralph Page. *The Country Dance Book: The Best of the Early Contras and Squares, Their History, Lore, Callers, Tunes, and Joyful Instructions.* Revised edition. Brattleboro, Vt.: The Stephen Green Press, 1976.

Nonprint resources

Johnson, Anne, and Susan Spalding. *Step Back Cindy: Old Time Dancing in Southwest Virginia.* Whitesburg, Ky.: Appalshop, Inc., 1990. Videocassette.

Seeger, Mike and Ruth Pershing. *Talking Feet: Solo Southern Dance - Buck, Flatfoot, and Tap.* El Cerrito, Calif.: Flower Films and Video, 1987. Videocassette.

Ballroom Dancing, Club Dancing, Competition Dancing, and Dance Sport

These styles of dancing include ballroom, competition, and club dancing, such as exhibition ballroom dance, disco, salsa, step dance, and Rave dance parties, and are all phenomena of the late twentieth century with roots in other cultural traditions. Books on these styles generally emerge after their peaks, and current studies are more readily found online and in the periodical literature. This list offers a survey of ballroom and club dancing as well as competition dancing and dance sport events covering the twentieth century, including some classic manuals. Not listed here are publications of the Fred Astaire Studios and Arthur Murray; inquire of local teaching establishments for latest editions. Since local tastes change very frequently, and local practices vary widely, seek advice for acquistions from those who are teaching locally. For information on vernacular dance, see the African, African American, and African Caribbean sections. See the sections on Dance Ethnology and the Anthropology of Dance, and Dance Theory for additional literature on cultural aspects of these phenomena.

Print resources

Ballroom Dance Music: A Reference Guide. New York: Gordon Press Publications, 1994.

Bottomer, Paul. *Line Dancing* (1996), *Mambo and Merengue* (1997), *Quickstep* (1997), *Samba and Lambada* (1997), *Rock'n' Roll* (1996), *Salsa* (1996), *Tango Argentino* (1996), *Waltz* (1997), Dance Crazy Series. London; New York: Lorenz Books.

Castle, Vernon and Irene. *Modern Dancing, by Mr. and Mrs. Vernon Castle, With Many Illustrations From Photographs and Moving Pictures of the Newest Dances for which the Authors Posed.* Introduction by Elisabeth Marbury. Reprint of the 1914 ed. New York: Da Capo Press, 1980.

Cressey, Paul Goalby. *The Taxi-Dance Hall; A Sociological Study in Commercialized Recreation and City Life.* New York: Greenwood Press, 1968, 1932.

    Facsimile reprint of edition issued by University of Chicago Press, 1932.

Dancing Fools and Weary Blues: The Great Escape of the Twenties. Edited by Lawrence R. Broer and John D. Walther. Bowling Green, Ohio: Bowling Green State University Popular Press, 1990.

Hill, Kathleen. *Dance for Physically Disabled Persons: A Manual for Teaching Ballroom, Square, and Folk Dances to Users of Wheelchairs and Crutches.* Washington, D.C., Physical Education and Recreation for the Handicapped; Information and Research Utilization Center, 1976.

Laird, Walter. *The Ballroom Dance Pack.* New York: Dorling Kindersley, 1993. Includes audio CD and 8 cards.

Leisner, Tony. *The Official Guide to Country Dance Steps.* Chicago: Domus Books, 1980.

Malbon, Ben. *Clubbing: Dancing, Ecstasy and Vitality.* London; New York: Routledge, 1999.

Malnig, Julie. *Dancing Till Dawn: A Century of Exhibition Ballroom Dance.* New York: Greenwood Press, 1992.

Ray, Ollie M. *Encyclopedia of Line Dances:The Steps That Came and Stayed.* Reston, Va.: National Dance Association, 1992.

Reynolds, John Lawrence. *Ballroom Dancing: The Romance, Rhythm and Style.* San Diego, Calif.: Laurel Glen, 1998.
> Includes listings of major North American and international dancesport events.

Silcott, Mireille. *Rave America: New School Dancescapes.* Toronto: ECW Press, 1999.

Silvester, Victor. *Modern Ballroom Dancing.* London: Stanley Paul, 1993.

Stephenson, Richard Montgomery and Joseph Iaccariono. *The Complete Book of Ballroom Dancing.* Garden City, N.Y. : Doubleday, 1980.
> Includes directions, with floor diagrams and photos, for dancing the American waltz, fox-trot, lindy, American rumba, cha-cha, mambo, tango, samba, bossa nova, merengue, ballroom polka, and hustle.

Vermey, Ruud. *Latin: Thinking, Sensing, and Doing in Latin American Dancing.* Munich: Kastell Verlag, 1994.

Western Outlaws. *Line Dance Steps.* North Shields: North Tyneside Libraries, 1996– .

Whitworth, Thomas Alan. *Modern Sequence Dancing for All.* Chesterfield, Derbyshire, U.K.: T. A.Whitworth, 1994.

———. *A History of Sequence Dancing and Script List.* Chesterfield, Derbyshire, U.K.: T.A. Whitworth, 1995.
> The text is based on a list of scripts compiled by Derek Guy ...revised and extended by Ken Fuller and others.

Wright, Judy Patterson. *Social Dance: Steps to Success.* Champaign, Ill.: Leisure Press, 1992.

Young, Tricia Henry. *Break All Rules!: Punk Rock and the Making of a Style*. Ann Arbor, Mich.: UMI Research Press, 1989.

Nonprint resources
Numerous series of instructional dance and ballroom competition videos are available. See *Dance on Camera, A Guide to Dance Films and Videos*, or ask local instructors for suggestions. Ballroom and dancesport periodicals often advertise videotapes of competitions and instructional methods.

Ballroom Dancing: The International Championships. New York: V.I.E.W. Video, 1991. Recorded in Ostrava, Czechoslovakia, in 1991. Videocassette.

Check Your Body at the Door. Compiled and directed by Sally Sommer. [publication pending]. Videocassette.
>   Documentary on underground club dancing beginning in the early 1990's.

Everybody Dance Now. New York: WNET/ Great Performances Dance in America, 1991. Videocassette.

Highlights of the Seventieth Blackpool Dance Festival. British Amateur Championships. Director, Peter Pember. Croton-on-Hudson, N.Y.: Quasar Video; distr. See-Do Productions, 1995. Videocassette.

Paris is Burning. Film: Prestige / Miramax / Off-White Productions, 1991. Videocassette: Academy Entertainment, 1992. Producer/ director: Jennie Livingston.
>   Documentary on drag balls, competitions that combine elements of dance, fashion, and mimicry of the straight world, held in New York transvestite clubs.

Variety Dance

This section includes monographs on minstrel, vaudeville and burlesque. The minstrel show is usually considered the first uniquely American show-business form. Minstrel shows were variety acts and included dance in addition to song, music and comic sketches. American vaudeville was a composite of variety of forms of entertainment including theatrical skits, comic skits, singing and dancing. A variety of dance styles were used in vaudeville which influenced many popular dance forms at the time. Burlesque was patterned after vaudeville and the minstrel show. Also a variety show, the finale was a performance by an exotic dancer or a wrestling or boxing match. See also the section on Biography and Autobiography for works on individuals, the sections on Jazz Dance, Tap Dance, and the African American section for other cultural, analytical, and historical references, and the section on Dance Theory for cultural aspects of this phenomena.

Minstrel

Print resources

Courlander, Harold. *Negro Folk Music, USA*. New York: Dover, 1992.

Emery, Lynne Fauley. *Black Dance: From 1619 to Today*. 2nd. rev. ed. Princeton, N.J. : Princeton Book Co. , 1988.

Fletcher, Tom. *100 Years of the Negro in Show Business*. Originally published 1954. New York : Da Capo Press, 1984 [1954].

Hughes, Langston. *Black Magic: A Pictorial History of the African-American in the Performing Arts*. New York: Da Capo Press, 1990.

Nathan, Hans. *Dan Emmett and the Rise of Early Negro Minstrelsy*. Norman, University of Oklahoma Press, 1962.

Riis, Thomas Lawrence. *More Than Just Minstrel Shows: The Rise of Black Musical Theatre at the Turn of the Century*. Brooklyn, N.Y.: Institute for Studies in American Music, Conservatory of Music, Brooklyn College of the City University of New York, 1992.

Sampson, Henry T. *Blacks in Blackface: A Source Book on Early Black Musical Shows*. Metuchen, N.J.: Scarecrow Press, 1980.

Stearns, Marshall Winslow and Jean Stearns. *Jazz Dance: The Story of American Vernacular Dance*. New York: Schirmer Books, 1979; rev. ed., Da Capo Press, 1994.

Toll, Robert C. *Blacking Up. The Minstrel Show in Nineteenth Century America*. Originally published 1974. New York: Oxford University Press, 1977.

———. *On With the Show!: The First Century of Show Business in America*. New York: Oxford University Press, 1976.

Wittke, Carl. *Tambo and Bones: A History of the American Minstrel Stage*. Originally published 1930. New York: Greenwood Press, 1968.

Nonprint resources

Spirit of Vaudeville. Black Minstrelsy. Series: Eye on dance ; 171. New York: ARC Videodance, 1985. Videocassette.

Vaudeville
Print resources

DiMeglio, John E. *Vaudeville U.S.A.* Bowling Green, Ohio: Bowling Green University Popular Press, 1973.

Gilbert, Douglas. *American Vaudeville It's Life and Times.* First published 1940. New York: Dover Publications, Inc. 1968.

Laurie, Joe. *Vaudeville: From the Honky-Tonks to the Palace.* New York: Holt, 1953.

Seldes, Gilbert. *The Seven Lively Arts.* New York: Sagamore Press Inc., 1957.

Smith, Bill. *The Vaudevillians.* New York: MacMillan, 1976.

Snyder, Robert W. *The Voice of the City: Vaudeville and Popular Culture in New York.* New York: Oxford University Press, 1989.

Sobel, Bernard. *Pictorial History of Vaudeville.* New York: Citadel Press, 1961.

Stein, Charles. *American Vaudeville As Seen By It's Contemporaries.* New York: Knopf, 1984.

Toll, Robert C. *On With the Show!: The First Century of Show Business in America.* NewYork: University of Oxford Press, 1976.

Nonprint resources

Spirit of Vaudeville. Rejuvenation of the Style. Series: Eye on Dance ; 169. New York: ARC Videodance, 1985. Video-cassette.

Spirit of Vaudeville. The Heart of Vaudeville. Series: Eye on Dance; 172. New York: ARC Videodance, 1985. Video-cassette.

Vaudeville: An American Masters Series. Produced by Rosemary Garner. KCTS-TV, 1997. Videocassette.

Burlesque
Print resources

Corio, Ann, and Joe DiMona. *This Was Burlesque.* New York: Grosset and Dunlap, 1968.

Green, William, "Strippers and Coochers—The Quintessence of American Burlesque" *Western Popular Theatre. The Proceedings of the Symposium Sponsored by the Manchester University Department of Drama*. Edited by David Mayer and Kenneth Richards. London: Methuen, 1977.

Lee, Gypsy Rose. *Gypsy*. Originally published 1957. London: Futura, 1988.

Minsky, Morton and Milt Machlin. *Minsky's Burlesque*. New York: Arbor House, 1986.

Sobel, Bernard. *Burleycue; An Underground History of Burlesque Days*. New York: Farrar & Rinehart, 1931.

———. *A Pictorial History of Burlesque*. New York: G.P. Putnam's Sons, 1956.

Zeidman, Irving. *American Burlesque Show*. New York: Hawthorne, 1967.

Nonprint resources

Gypsy. Directed by Mervyn LeRoy. Based on the memoirs of Gypsy Rose Lee. Warner Home Video; 1984 [1962]. Videocassette.

The Night They Raided Minsky's. Based on the novel by Rowland Barber. MGM/UA Home Video. 1991 [1968]. Videocassette.

Here It Is, Burlesque! Produced by Michael Brandman. Vestron Video; Stamford, Conn. 1979. Videocassette.

Dance in Commercial Theater and Movies, including Broadway and Hollywood Musicals

Included in this section are works related to the development of dance within commercial theater and broadcast media. Musical theater dates back to the eighteenth century, but musical theater dance came into its own on America's Broadway stage. Dance on film, technically created at the end of the nineteenth century, with the development of television and film in America commercial broadcast media became a major cultural phenomenon in the twentieth century. Dance in commercial theater and broadcast media has developed into a unique dance tradition with many forms, styles and traditions imbedded in the choreography. See also the section on Biography and Autobiography for works on individual film dancers. A list of popular dance movies from Hollywood and international cinema is included as a separate sub-section. See also the section on Dance Biographies and Autobiographies for related sources.

Print resources

Billman, Larry. *Film Choreographers and Dance Directors: A Heavily-Illustrated Biographical Encyclopedia with A History and Filmographies, 1893-1995.* Jefferson, N.C.: McFarland and Co., 1996.

Delamater, Jerome. *Dance in the Hollywood Musical.* Ann Arbor, Mich.: UMI Research Press, c.1981.

Kislan, Richard. *The Musical: A Look at the American Musical Theater.* Rev. expanded ed. New York: Applause Theatre Book Publishers, 1995.

Kobal, John. *Gotta Sing, Gotta Dance : A History of Movie Musicals.* Rev. ed. New York: Exeter Books ; distributed by Bookthrift, 1983.

Mueller, John E. *Astaire Dancing: The Musical Films.* New York: Knopf, 1985.

Parker, David and Esther Siegel. *Guide to Dance in Film.* Detroit, Mich.: Gale Research Company, 1978.

Porter, Susan L. *With an Air Debonair: Musical Theatre in America, 1785-1815.* Washington, D.C.: Smithsonian Institution Press, 1991.

Prevots, Naima. *Dancing in the Sun: Hollywood Choreographers, 1915-1937.* Ann Arbor, Mich.: UMI Research Press, 1987.

Schlundt, Christena L. *Dance in the Musical Theater: Jerome Robbins and His Peers: A Guide.* New York: Garland, 1989.

Nonprint resources

That's Dancing. Produced by Metro-Golwyn-Mayer. Culver City, Calif.: MGM/UA Home Video, 1991, 1985. Videocassette. Compendium of dance from Hollywood musical films.

Following is a "highlights" list of some of the great dance movies from Hollywood and international cinema. Many can be purchased through standard video distributors.

All That Jazz
An American in Paris
Anchors Aweigh
Anything Goes
Babes in Arms
Band Wagon
Blood Wedding
The Boy Friend
Brigadoon
Bye Bye Birdie
Cabaret
Call Me Madam
Carnival of Rhythm
Carousel
The Court Jester
Cover Girl
Damn Yankees
Dancin'
Dirty Dancing
Down Argentine Way
Fame
Fiddler on the Roof
Finnegan's Rainbow
Flamenco
Flashdance
Flying Down to Rio
Follow the Fleet
Footlight Parade
42nd Street
Funny Face
The Gang's All Here
Goldwyn Folies of 1935
Good News
Guys and Dolls
Hair
Hans Christian Andersen

Holiday Inn
I Was an Adventuress
Isadora
Kismet
Kiss Me Kate
The Little Colonel
The Music Man
Nijinsky
Oklahoma
On the Town
On Your Toes
Pal Joey
Paris is Burning
Pennies From Heaven
The Pirate
The Red Shoes
Royal Wedding
Saturday Night Fever
Seven Brides for Seven Brothers
Silk Stockings
Singing in the Rain
Stormy Weather
Strictly Ballroom
Sweet Charity
Swing Time
Take Me Out to the Ball Game
Tap
That's Entertainment!
Top Hat
The Turning Point
West Side Story
White Christmas
White Nights
The Wiz
The Wizard of Oz
Yankee Doodle Dandy

Television and Video Dance
Monographs in this area are few. See periodical literature indexes to locate articles on dance in television, music videos and MTV, and dance for the camera. See also the *International Encyclopedia of Dance* articles, "Film and Video: Choreography for the Camera," and "Television." See also Modern and Postmodern Dance, and Dance Theory for related sources.

Print resources
Jordan, Stephanie, and David Allen, eds. *Parallel Lines: Media Representations of Dance.* London: Arts Council of Great Britain and John Libbey and Co., 1993.
Prince, Harold. *Contradictions: Notes on Twenty-six Years in the Theatre.* New York: Dodd, Mead, 1974.
Rose, Brian G. *Television and the Performing Arts: A Handbook and Reference Guide to American Cultural Programming.* New York: Greenwood, 1986.

Nonprint resources
See also index listings under the subject "Experimental" and series "Alive from Off Center" in *Dance on Camera: A Guide to Dance Films and Videos.* Lanham, Md.: Scarecrow Press and New York: Neal-Schuman Publishers, 1998.
Dance on Television and Film: Dance and the New Music Videos [Eye on Dance; 110] Videocassette. New York: ARC Videodance, 1984.
Dance on Television and Film: Creating Dance for the Camera [Eye on Dance; 148] Videocassette. New York: ARC Videodance, 1985.
Dance on Television and Film: Effective Approaches [Eye on Dance; 196] Videocassette. New York: ARC Videodance, 1986.
Everybody Dance Now. Videocassette. [New York]: WNET/ Great Performances Dance in America, 1991.

Choreography instruction is extremely rare compared to technique instruction, and even less has been published about how to do it. This list pulls together the few manuals available, and balances them with several expositions by choreographers of their process on videotape and CD-ROM. In addition to this section, readers interested in choreographic methods should explore the section on Dance Biographies and Autobiographies, where books by choreographers provide information on choreographic process. See also the section on Dance Notation, and the section on Dance Theory for related sources.

Print resources

Albright, Ann Cooper. *Choreographing Difference: The Body and Identity in Contemporary Dance*. Hanover, N.H.: University Press of New England, 1997.

Berkson, Robert. *Musical Theater Choreography: a Practical Method for Preparing and Staging Dance in a Musical Show*. New York: Back Stage Books, 1990.

Cunningham, Merce. *The Dancer and the Dance: In Conversation with Jacqueline Lesschaeve*. New York: M. Boyars, distr. by Scribner Book Co., 1985; rev. and updated, M. Boyars, distr. by Rizzoli, 1991.

Footnotes: Six Choreographers Inscribe the Page, essays, Douglas Dunn, Marjorie Gamso, Ishmael Houston-Jones, Yvonne Meier, Sara Skaggs; text and commentary Elena Alexander; foreward Jill Johnston. Amsterdam: G + B Arts International, 1998.

Halprin, Anna. *Moving Toward Life: Five Decades of Transformational Dance*. Hanover, N.H.: University Press of New England, 1995.

Hawkins, Erick. *The Body Is a Clear Place and Other Statements on Dance*, with an introd. by Alan M. Kriegsman. Princeton, N.J.: Princeton Book Company, 1992.

Hay, Deborah. *Lamb at the Altar: The Story of a Dance*, with photographs by Phyllis Liedeker. Durham, N.C.: Duke University Press, 1994.

Hodes, Stuart. *A Map of Making Dances*. New York: Ardsley House Publishers, 1998.

Horst, Louis. *Pre-Classic Dance Forms.* New York: Dance Observer, 1937; reprint, with an introd. by Janet Soares, Princeton, N.J.: Princeton Book Co., 1987.

Humphrey, Doris. *The Art of Making Dances*, ed. by Barbara Pollack. New York: Rinehart, 1959; Princeton, N.J.: A Dance Horizons Book, Princeton Book Co., 1959, 1987.

Jones, Bill T., and Arnie Zane. *Body Against Body: The Dance and Other Collaborations.* Elizabeth Zimmer and Susan Quasha, eds. Barrytown, N.Y.: Station Hill Press, 1989.

Lawson, Jane. *Ballet-Maker's Handbook: Sources, Vocabulary, Styles.* London: A. & C. Black; New York: Routledge/Theatre Arts Books, 1991.

Minton, Sandra Cerny. *Choreography: A Basic Approach to Using Improvisation.* Champaign, Ill.: Human Kinetics Press, 1997.

Nagrin, Daniel. *Dance and the Specific Image: Improvisation.* Pittsburgh: University of Pittsburgh Press, 1994.

The Notebooks of Martha Graham. With an introd. by Nancy Wilson Ross. New York: Harcourt Brace Jovanovich, 1973.

Shay, Anthony. *Choreophobia: Solo Improvised Dance in the Iranian World.* Costa Mesa, Calif: Mazda Publishers, 1999.

Tufnell, Miranda and Chris Crickmay. *Body, Space, Image: Notes Towards Improvisation and Performance.* London: Virago, 1990.

Van Pragh, Peggy and Peter Brinson. *The Choreographic Art: An Outline of Its Principles and Craft.* New York: Alfred A. Knopf, 1963.

Wigman, Mary. *The Language of Dance*, ed. and transl. by Walter Sorell. Middletown, Conn.: Wesleyan University Press, 1966, distr. Books on Demand (UMI).

Nonprint resources

Bessie: A Portrait of Bessie Schönberg, prod. and dir. Chris Hegedus and D.A. Pennebaker, 58 min., Pennebaker Hegedus Films, 1999. Videocassette.

> Portrait of the master teacher of choreographic workshops working with students.

Chance Favors the Prepared Mind, prod. Vlaams Theaterinstituut, Ministerie van Ouderwijs dienst Media en Informatie, dir. Anne Quirynen, 25 min. 1990. Videocassette.

> Explorations by William Forsythe and four Frankfurt Ballet dancers in finding movement ideas for choreography.

Contact, prod. Ann Tegnell and Susan Warner, 22 min., Temple University, 1979. Videocassette.

> Introduction to the principles of contact improvisation as a physical technique and choreographic tool.

Creative Process: Personal and Creative Growth, (Eye on Dance, 258), prod. Celia Ipiotis and Jeff Bush, 28 min., ARC Videodance, 1988. Videocassette.

> Clark Tippett and Kevin McKenzie of American Ballet Theatre discuss balancing their contributions as dancers and choreographers.

Dance as an Art Form, prod. Jack Lieb Productions, dir. and chor. Murray Louis, 150 min, Chimera Foundation for the Arts, 1972-73. Videocassette.

> Five part series on the elements of choreography. Individual segments are titled *The Body as an Instrument, Motion, Space, Time, Shape*.

The Immortals: An Adventure in Ballet Reconstruction. prod. Ausdance Western Australia, 1992. Videocassette.

> Reconstructions of a 1939 ballet by Linley Wilson.

Making Dances: Seven Post Modern Choreographers, prod. and dir. Michael Blackwood, written by Marcia B. Siegel, 89 min., Michael Blackwood Productions, 1980. Videocassette.

> Works and creative methods of Meredith Monk, Trisha Brown, Lucinda Childs, Douglas Dunn, David Gordon, Kenneth King, and Sara Rudner.

Martha Clarke: Light and Dark, prod. Joyce Chopra, dir. Martha Clarke and Joyce Chopra, 54 min., WNET/Thirteen, distr. Phoenix/BFA Films, 1981. Videocassette.

> Examination of the artist's sources and process in a duet with Felix Blaska.

Twyla Tharp: Making Television Dance, prod. Twyla Tharp Dance Foundation and WNET/Thirteen, 58 min., distr. Phoenix/BFA Films, 1978. Videocassette.

> Tharp, with Mikhail Baryshnikov, analyzes her dances and how to use the visual vocabulary of television.

What Do Pina Bausch and Her Dancers Do in Wupperthal? prod. NDR and Westdeutsches Fernsehen, dir. Kaus Wildenhahn, 115 min., Inter Nationes, 1983. Videocassette.

> Documentary on Pina Bausch filmed during rehearsals for *Walzer*.

William Forsythe: Improvisation Technologies. A Tool for the Analytical Dance Eye. ZKM Karlsruhe and Deutsches Tanzarchiv, Cologne/ SK Stiftung Kultur. CD-ROM (Mac/PC), English language. Issued with a booklet in English and German, text by Roslyn Sulcas and interview with William Forsythe.

Dance Production and Administration

Included in this section are books, videos, periodical literature and new media which contain information related to the technical and administrative production of concert dance for professional venues that stage and produce dance, including sources on auditions, staging, direction, lighting, sound, costume, and make-up. Though not appropriate for most sections in this bibliography, technical manuals and handbooks, as well as practical guides and other instructional resources are represented, given the very nature of technical dance production. As the literature of production and administration overlap, current sources related to the administration of professional dance production are also included in this section. Some selections are not specific to dance but generally applicable to stage production and administration. See also the section on Dance and Related Arts.

Print resources

Barrell, M. Kay. *The Technical Production Handbook: Guide for Performing Arts Presenting Organizations and Touring Companies.* Santa Fe, N.M.: Western States Arts Federation, 1991.

Berkson, Robert. *Musical Theatre Choreography: A Practical Method for Preparing and Staging Dance in a Musical Show.* New York: Back Stage Books, 1990.

Boulanger, Norman C. *Theatre Lighting A to Z.* Seattle: University of Washington Press, 1992.

Clarke, Mary, and Clement Crisp. *Design for Ballet.* New York: Hawthorn Books, 1978.

Cook, Ray. *A Handbook for the Dance Director.* New York: Ray Cook, 1977, rev. ed., 1981.

Cooper, Susan. *Staging Dance.* New York: Theatre Arts Books/ Routledge, 1998.

Downs, Harold. *Theatre and Stage: An Encyclopaedic Guide to the Performance of All Amateur Dramatic, Operatic, and Theatrical Work.* London: Pitman, 1974.

Drydan, Deborah. *Fabric Painting and Dyeing for the Theater.* Westport, Conn.: Heinemann, 1993.

Ellfeldt, Lois. *Dance Production Handbook; or, Later Is Too Late.* Palo Alto, Calif.: National Press Books, 1971.

Engel, Lehman. *Planning and Producing the Musical Show*. New York: Crown Publishers, 1957.

Fraser, Neil. *Lighting and Sound*. London: Phaidon Press, 1995.

A Guide to Dance Production: "On With the Show". Reston, Va.: AAPHERD, 1981.

Holt, Michael. *Costume and Make-Up*. London: Phaidon Press, 1995.

———. *Stage Design and Properties*. London: Phaidon Press, 1995.

International Directory of Design. 8, Film, Photography, Video, Theatrical & Set Design. 5th ed. San Francisco: Penrose Press, 2000.

Joiner, Betty. *Costumes for the Dance*. New York: A.S. Barnes, 1937.

Jowers, Sidney Jackson, and John Cavanagh. *Theatrical Costume, Make-up and Wigs: A Bibliography and Iconography*. London and New York: Routledge, 2000.

Lord, William H. *Stagecraft: A Complete Guide to Backstage Work*. Colorado Springs, Colo.: Merriweather Publishing, 2000.

Menear, Pauline and Terry Hawkins. *Stage Management and Theater Administration*, reprint, rev. London: Phaidon Press, 1995.

Pectal, Lynn. *Costume Design: Techniques of Modern Masters*. New York: Watson-Guptill Publications, 1999.

Poor Dancer's Almanac: Managing Life and Work in the Performing Arts.. Compiled by the Dance Theater Workshop, David R. White, Lise Friedman, and Tia Tibbitts Levinson., eds. Durham, N.C.: Duke University Press, 1993.

Rey, Frank. *The Annual Dance Recital (Concert): Blood and Sequins*. Waldwick, N.J.: Hector, 1978.

Russell, William R., ed. *Life on the Road: A Beginner's Guide to the Stage Production Touring Industry*. 3rd ed., Boston: Pearson Custom Publishing, 1996.

Schlaich, Joan, and Betty DuPont. *Dance: The Art of Production*, 2nd. ed. Princeton, N.J.: Princeton Book Company, 1988.

Sherbon, Elizabeth. *On the Count of One: The Art, Craft, and Science of Teaching Modern Dance*. Pennington, N.J.: A Cappella Books, 1990.

Skeel, Suzanne. *Recital Recipes: The Teacher's Guide to Recital Production and Management*. Philadelphia: Susan Skeel, 1991.

Strand-Evans, Katherine. *Costume Construction*. Prospect Heights, Ill.: Waveland Press, 1999.

Waine, Graham. *Projection for the Performing Arts*. Woburn, Mass.: Butterworth-Heinemann, 1995.

Williams, Peter. *Masterpieces of Ballet Design*. London: Phaidon Press, 1981.

Wolfram, Eric. *Your Dance Resume: a Preparatory Guide to the Audition*. San Francisco: Macmillan, 1994.

Dance Notation

Many choreographers and dancers have recorded their works, albeit imperfectly, using words, pictures, or symbols. Film and video increasingly are used, but the camera presents its own problems when documenting dance. Since the fifteenth century, a handful of notation systems have been used. The Renaissance and Baroque section of this volume presents examples of the major pre-nineteenth century Western European notation systems. In the nineteenth and twentieth century, over a hundred new notation systems were introduced, but few are in widespread use. In Western countries, two systems, Benesh notation and Labanotation are widely known and taught in institutional settings. This section includes both the frequently used and more obscure notation systems, and is subdivided into four parts: notation surveys, nineteenth century, twentieth century notation guides, and twentieth century published Labanotation scores. English translations are cited whenever possible. Unpublished works known only in manuscript are not included, nor are periodical articles, advanced study guides, workbooks, or conference papers. These, however, should be consulted for in-depth research . Notation software is included in a sub-section of the non-print resources listing, complete with URL addresses for downloading.

Print resources
NOTATION SURVEYS
Guest, Ann Hutchinson. *Choreo-Graphics: A Comparison of Dance Notation Systems from the Fifteenth Century to the Present.* New York: Gordon and Breach, 1989.

Guest, Ann Hutchinson. *Dance Notation: the Process of Recording Movement on Paper.* London: Dance Books, 1984.

Jeschke, Claudia. *Tanzschriften: ihre geschichte une methode.* Publikationen des Instituts für Musikwissenschaft der Universität Salzburg. Derra de Moroda Dance Archives Tanzforschungen II. Bad Reichenhall: Comes Verlag, 1983.

NINETEENTH CENTURY NOTATION INSTRUCTION AND GUIDES
Saint-Léon, Arthur M. *La sténochorégraphie ou art d'écrire proprement la danse.* Paris: chez l'auteur, 1852. Modern edition of notation

sections only, transl. by Raymond Lister: *Stenochoreography, or The Art of Writing Dancing Swiftly*. Cambridge: distr. Deighton Bell & Co., [1994].

Stepanov, Vladimir Ivanovich. *Alphabet of Movements of the Human Body: A Study in Recording the Movements of the Human Body by Means of Musical Signs*. Translated by Raymond Lister from the French edition of 1892. New York: Dance Horizons, c.1969.

Zorn, Friedrich Albert. *Grammar of the Art of Dancing Theoretical and Practical: Lessons in the Arts of Dancing and Dance Writing (Choreography)*. Translated from the German of the original Leipzig edition, 1887. Edited by Alfonso Josephs Sheafe. Modern rev. ed. New York: Burt Franklin, 1977.

TWENTIETH CENTURY NOTATION INSTRUCTION AND GUIDES

Beck, Jill and Joseph Reiser. *Moving Notation: A Handbook of Musical Rhythm and Elementary Labanotation for the Dancer*. Performing Arts Studies Vol. 6. Amsterdam: Harwood Academic Publishers, 1998.

> Includes compact disk, *Introduction to Labanotation*, with assignments.

Benesh, Rudolf and Joan. *Reading Dance: the Birth of Choreology*. A Condor Book. London: Souvenir Press (E. & A.) Ltd., 1977.

Borgo, Frances and Virginia. *The Borgo Method. Tap Shorthand: A Fast and Easy Way to Write Tap Steps and Combinations*. Royal Oak, Mich.: Borgo Sisters, 1993–4.

Dell, Cecily. *A Primer for Movement Description: Using Effort-Shape and Supplementary Concepts*. 2nd ed. New York: Dance Notation Bureau, 1970.

Eshkol, Noa and Wachmann, Abraham. *Movement Notation*. London: Weidenfeld and Nicholson, 1958.

Guest, Ann Hutchinson. *Your Move: A New Approach to the Study of Movement and Dance*. New York : Gordon and Breach, c.1983. 3 vols.

———. *Labanotation or Kinetography Laban: the System of Analyzing and Recording Movement*. 3rd ed. revised. New York: Routledge, 1987.

Knust, Albrecht. *A Dictionary of Kinetography Laban (Labanotation)*. Volume 1 Text, Volume 2, Examples. Princeton, N.J.: Princeton Book Company, 1976.

McGuinness-Scott, Julia. *Movement Study and Benesh Movement Notation.* London: Oxford University Press, 1983.

Miles, Alan. *Dictionary of Classical Ballet in Labanotation.* Princeton, N.J.: Princeton Book Company, 1976.

Sutton, Valerie. *DanceWritingSite*, includes publications. http://www.DanceWriting.org/

Topaz, Muriel. *Elementary Labanotation: A Study Guide.* With a chapter on Motif Description by Odette Blum., the author, 1996.

Topaz, Muriel and Jane Marriet. *Study Guide for Intermediate Labanotation.* 2nd ed. New York: Dance Notation Bureau Press, 1986.

U Chang Sop. *The Chamo System of Dance Notation.* Foreign Languages Publishing House. Pyongyang, Korea, 1988. (In English and Korean)

TWENTIETH CENTURY PUBLISHED LABANOTATION SCORES

Doris Humphrey: The Collected Works. New York: Dance Notation Bureau Press, 1978–

Language of Dance Series. Lausaanne: Gordon and Breach, 1987–
　　1. *The Flower Festival in Genzano: Pas de Deux* 2. *Shawn's Fundamentals of Dance* 3. *Nijinsky's Faune Restored* 4. *Tudor's Soiree Musicale* 5. *Ballade by Anna Sokolow* 6. *La Vivandiere Pas de Six* 7. *Robert le Diable The Ballet of the Nuns*

The Educational Performance Collection Series. New York: Dance Notation Bureau, 1985–
　　Rachel Lampert's *What's Remembered?*; Buzz Miller's *Not For Love Alone*; Moses Pendleton's *Children On the Hill*; Clay Taliaferro's *Falling Off the Back Porch.* (Package includes notation score, critical analysis, videotape and performance rights.)

Nahumck, Nadia Chilkovsky. *Isadora Duncan: The Dances.* Nicholas Nahumck, autographer, assisted by Anne M. Moll. Washington, D.C.: National Museum of Women in the Arts, 1994. With additional assistance from Hortense Kooluris and Julia Levien for dance research, Harry Hewitt for music research....Fully reviewed by the Dance Notation Bureau.

　　Contains dances and dance exercises by Isadora Duncan and her protegés recorded in Labanotation. Includes biblio-

graphical references (530–32) and list of music sources for
selected Duncan dances (524–29).

Venable, Lucy, and Fred Berk. *Ten Folk Dances in Labanotation.* New
York : M. Witmark, 1959.

Nonprint resources

Intensive Course in Elementary Labanotation 5 videocassettes.
Hightstown, N.J. : Princeton Book Company, c.1988.
Nine classroom lessons presented by instructor Jill Beck. An
accompanying study guide is available.

The Alphabetic Symbols for Dance Notation. Korean Scientific and
Educational Studio, 1988?] Videocassette 1. Korean language
version. Videocassette 2. English language version.
Accompanies U Chang Sop's book The Chamo system of
dance notation (1988).

Videotapes to accompany *The Educational Performance Collection
Series.* New York: Dance Notation Bureau, 1985–

COMPUTER SOFTWARE

Calaban. Adamson, Andy. Department of Drama and Theatre Arts,
The University of Birmingham, P.O. Box 363, Birmingham B15
2TT.
PC software for writing Labanotation

LabanWriter. Available at the World Wide Web site of Ohio State
University—http://www.dance.ohio-state.edu/files/
LabanWriter/index.html.
Macintosh software for writing Labanotation.

Life Forms 3 for Windows 95/98/NT and Macintosh. Demonstration
version at www.credo-interactive.com/downloads/
downloads.html.

MacBenesh http://members.home.net/dancewrite/index.htm
Macintosh software for writing Benesh Notation

Motographicon (Rajka Movement Notation) Movement design
described and demonstrated at www.speech.kth.se/kacor/
projects/kinetics.htm.

DANCE CRITICISM

Collections of dance criticism have appeared in book form over the past thirty years, but many of these are now out of print. Other influential dance critics have never been published in book form. The books listed here are the best collected works available, and a few theoretical studies by and about important critics. However, it should be noted that much dance criticism can be located only via newspaper and periodical indexes, and that the criticism of smaller newspapers may not be indexed, yet may contain the only reviews of significant emerging artists. See also the sections on Ballet, Modern and Postmodern Dance, and Dance Theory.

Print resources

Anderson, Jack. *Choreography Observed.* Iowa City: University of Iowa Press, 1987.

Banes, Sally. *Writing Dancing in the Age of Postmodernism.* Hanover, N.H.: Wesleyan University Press, University Press of New England, 1994.

Buckle, Richard. *Buckle at the Ballet.* London: Dance Books, 1980.

Connor, Lynne. *Spreading the Gospel of the Modern Dance: Newspaper Dance Criticism in the United States, 1850–1934.* Pittsburgh: University of Pittsburgh Press, 1997.

Croce, Arlene. *Afterimages.* New York: Alfred A. Knopf, 1977.

———. *Going to the Dance.* New York: Alfred A. Knopf, 1982.

———. *Sight Lines.* New York: Alfred A. Knopf, 1987.

———. *Writing in the Dark: Dancing in The New Yorker.* New York: Farrar, Straus & Giroux, 2000.

> An anthology which includes selections from the earlier books and more recent writings.

Denby, Edwin. *Dance Writings,* ed. by Robert Cornfield and William Mackay. New York: Alfred A. Knopf, 1986. Subsequently, *Dance Writings and Poetry.* New Haven: Yale University Press, 1998.

> Contains Denby's earlier collections *Looking at the Dance* and *Dancers, Buildings, and People in the Streets,* plus additional essays and reviews.

Foster, Susan Leigh. *Reading Dancing: Bodies and Subjects in Contemporary American Dance.* Berkeley: University of California Press, 1986.

Gautier, Théophile. *Gautier on Dance*, ed. and transl. by Ivor Guest. London: Dance Books, distr. by Princeton Book Co. 1986.
  Collected criticism of Théophile Gautier about the Romantic ballet in 19th century Paris.

Gere, David, Lewis Segal, Patrick Koelsch and Elizabeth Zimmer, eds. *Looking Out: Perspectives on Dance and Criticism in a Multicultural World*. Old Tappan, N.J.: MacMillan Library Reference, 1995.

Johnston, Jill. *Marmalade Me*. New York: E.P. Dutton and Co., 1971; Hanover, N.H.: University Press of New England, 1998.
  Selected writings from 1960–1970.

Jowitt, Deborah. *Dance Beat: Selected Views and Reviews, 1967–1976*. New York: Marcel Dekker, 1977; Ann Arbor, Mich.: Books on Demand (UMI).

———. *The Dance in Mind: Profiles and Reviews, 1976–1983*, with photographs by Lois Greenfield. Boston: D.R. Godine, 1985.

Levinson, André. *André Levinson on Dance: Writings from Paris in the Twenties*, ed. and with an introd. by Joan Acocella and Lynn Garafola. Hanover, N.H.: Wesleyan University Press, University Press of New England, 1991.

Martin, John Joseph, and Jack Anderson. *The Dance in Theory*, with new introd. by Jack Anderson. Princeton, N.J.: Princeton Book Co., 1989.

Morris, Gay, ed. *Moving Words: Re-writing Dance*. New York: Routledge, 1996.

Siegel, Marcia. *At the Vanishing Point*. New York: Saturday Review Press, 1972.

———. *The Tail of the Dragon: 1976–1987*. Durham, N.C.: Duke University Press, 1991

———. *Watching the Dance Go By*. Boston: Houghton-Mifflin, 1977. o.p.

Sorell, Walter. *Looking Back in Wonder: Diary of a Dance Critic*. New York: Columbia University Press, 1986.

Theodores, Diana. *First We Take Manhattan: Four American Women and the New York School of Dance Criticism*. Newark, N.J.: Gordon and Breach, 1996.
  A study of Deborah Jowitt, Arlene Croce, Marcia Siegel, and Nancy Goldner.

Van Vechten, Carl. *The Dance Writings of Carl Van Vechten*, ed. and with introd. by Paul Padgette. New York: Dance Horizons, 1974.

Nonprint resources

The Dance Critic's Role (Eye on Dance, 91), prod. Celia Ipiotis and
Jeff Bush, 29 min., ARC Videodance, 1983. Videocassette.
Discussion with critics Burt Supree, Linda Winer, and
Francis Mason.

Success and Demise of Dance Publications (Eye on Dance, 181), prod.
Celia Ipiotis and Jeff Bush, 29 min., ARC Videodance, 1986.
Videocassette.
William Como, Karl Reuling, and Marcia B. Siegel discuss
the readership, history, and economics of dance publishing,
including *Dance Magazine.*

Dance Theory

In the past decade, a large body of scholarship has emerged in the
area of dance and performance within theoretical perspectives,
linking dance with other disciplines in the humanities and social
sciences. New curricula in this area has been developed as well. This
section contains sources on theoretical approaches to dance and
dance research, including works on dance and philosophical, psychological, political, social, economic theory , as well as literature on race,
gender, ethnicity, and other cultural representations in dance. See
also the Dance Styles, Forms, and Traditions, Dance Ethnology and
the Anthropology of Dance, Dance Criticism, Dance Education, and
Somatic Studies sections.

Print resources

Adair, Christy. *Women and Dance: Sylphs and Sirens.* London:
Macmillan, 1992.
> Women in society.

Allen, Richard James, and Karen Pearlman, eds. *Performing the
Unnameable: An Anthology of Australian Performance Texts.*
Sydney: Curreney Press, 1999.

Alter, Judith B. *Dance-Based Dance Theory: from Borrowed Models to
Dance-Based Experience.* New Studies in Aesthetics, v. 7. New
York: P. Lang, 1991.

Banes, Sally. *Writing Dancing in the Age of Postmodernism.*
Middletown, Conn.: Wesleyan University Press; Hanover, N.H.:
University Press of New England, 1994.

———. *Democracy's Body: Judson Dance Theater, 1962-1964.* Durham,
N.C.: Duke University Press, 1993.

———. *Greenwich Village 1963: Avant-Garde Performance and the
Effervescent Body.* Durham: Duke University Press, 1993.
> Aesthetics, modern arts, popular culture in New York
> City.

Batchelard, Gaston. *The Poetics of Space.* Boston: Beacon Press,
reprint 1994.

Battcock, Gregory. *Performance Art.* New York: NAL/Dutton, 1984.

———. *Minimal Art: A Critical Anthology.* Berkeley: University of
California Press, 1995.

Bell Hooks see Hooks, Bell.

Birringer, Johannes H. *Theatre, Theory, Postmodernism*. Bloomington: Indiana University Press, 1991.

———. *Media and Performance: Along the Border*. Baltimore: Johns Hopkins Press, 1998.

Blackmer, Joan Dexter. *Acrobats of the Gods: Dance and Transformation*. Studies in Jungian Psychology by Jungian Analysts, 39. Toronto: Inner City Books, 1989.

Brown, Jean Morrison, Naomi Mindlin, and Charles H. Woodford, eds. *The Vision of Modern Dance in the Words of Its Creators*. Hightstown, N.J.: Princeton Book Company, 1998.

Browning, Barbara. *Infectious Rhythm: Metaphors of Contagion and the Spread of African Culture*. New York: Routledge, 1998.

———. *Samba: Resistance in Motion*. Bloomington: Indiana University Press, 1995.

Burt, Ramsay. *The Male Dancer: Bodies, Spectacle, Sexualities*. London, New York: Routledge, 1995.

Carlson, Marvin A. *Performance: A Critical Introduction*. London: New York: Routledge, 1996.

Case, Sue-Ellen, Philip Brett, and Susan Leigh Foster. *Cruising the Performative : Interventions into the Representation of Ethnicity, Nationality, and Sexuality*. Bloomington: Indiana University Press, 1995.

Certeau, Michel de. *The Practice of Everyday Life*. Steven F. Randall, trans. Berkeley: University of California Press, 1984.

Cass, Joan B. *Dancing Through History*. Englewood Cliffs, N.J.: Prentice Hall, 1993.

Cohen, Selma Jeanne. *Next Week, Swan Lake: Reflections on Dance and Dances*. Middletown, Conn.: Wesleyan University Press, 1982.

———, ed. *The Modern Dance: Seven Statements of Belief*. Middletown, Conn.: Wesleyan University Press, 1969, 1966.

———, ed. *Dance as a Theatre Art: Source Readings in Dance History from 1581 to the Present*. 2nd ed., Middletown, Conn.: Wesleyan University Press, 1992.

Copeland, Roger, and M. Cohen, eds. *What is Dance? Readings in Theory and Criticism*. Oxford: Oxford University Press, 1983.

Desmond, Jane. *Meaning in Motion: New Cultural Studies of Dance*. Durham, N.C.: Duke University Press, 1997.

Dewey, John. *Art as Experience.* New York: Minton, Balch & Co., 1934.

Diamond, Elin, ed. *Performance and Cultural Politics.* London/New York: Routledge, 1996.

Erickson, Jon. *The Fate of the Object : From Modern Object to Postmodern Sign in Performance, Art, and Poetry.* Ann Arbor, Mich.: University of Michigan Press, 1995.

Fancher, G., and G. Myers, eds. *Philosophical Essays on Dance.* Brooklyn, N.Y.: Dance Horizons, 1981.

Felshin, Nina, ed. *But Is It Art?: The Spirit of Art as Activism.* Seattle: Bay Press, 1995.

Foster, Susan Leigh ed.*Choreographing History.* Bloomington: Indiana University Press, 1995.

Franklin, Eric N. *Dynamic Alignment through Imagery.* Champaign, Ill.: Human Kinetics, 1996.

Franko, Mark. *Dance as Text: Ideologies of the Baroque Body.* Cambridge, Eng., New York: Cambridge University Press, 1993. (RES Monographs on Anthropology and Aesthetics)

———. *Dancing Modernism/Performing Politics.* Bloomington: Indiana University Press, 1995.

Franko, Mark, and Annette Richards, eds. *Acting on the Past: Historical Performance Across the Disciplines.* Hanover, N.H.: University Press of New England, 2000.

———. *Performance: Live Art Since 1960.* New York: Harry N. Abrams, 1998.

Fraleigh, Sondra Horton. *Dance and the Lived Body: a Descriptive Aesthetics.* Pittsburgh: University of Pittsburgh Press, 1987.

Fraleigh, Sondra Horton and Penelope Hanstein. *Researching Dance: Evolving Modes of Inquiry.* Pittsburgh: University of Pittsburgh Press, 1999.

Gere, David, ed. *Looking Out: Perspectives On Dance and Criticism in a Multicultural World.* Dance Critics Association. New York: Schirmer Books; London: Prentice Hall International, 1995.

Goellner, Ellen W., and Jacqueline Shea Murphy, eds. *Bodies of the Text: Dance as Theory, Literature as Dance.* New Brunswick, N.J.: Rutgers University Press, 1995.

Goldberg, RoseLee. *Performance Art: From Futurism to the Present.* Rev. and enl. ed. New York: Harry N. Abrams; London: Thames & Hudson, 1988.

Greenberg, Clement. *The Collected Essays and Criticism v.4; Modernism with a Vengeance, 1957-1969*. Chicago: University of Chicago Press, 1986.

Hein, Hilde, and Carolyn Korsmeyer, eds. *Aesthetics in Feminist Perspective*. Bloomington: Indiana University Press, 1993.

Highwater, Jamake. *Dance: Rituals of Experience*. 3rd ed. Pennington, N.J.: Princeton Book Co., 1992.

Hodgins, Paul. *Relationships Between Score and Choreography in Twentieth-Century Dance: Music, Movement and Metaphor*. Lewis, N.Y.: E. Mellen Press, 1992.

Hooks, Bell. *Black Looks: Race and Representation*. New York: Routledge, 1992.
> The chapters "Selling Hot Pussy," "Is Paris Burning," and "Madonna", deal with women, race and performance representation.

Huxley, Michael, and Noel Witts, eds. *The Twentieth Century Performance Reader*. London: New York: Routledge, 1996.

Johnston, Charles. *The Creative Imperative*. Berkeley, Calif: Celestial Jarts, 1986.

Jordan, Stephanie. *Striding Out: Aspects of Contemporary and New Dance in Britain*. London: Dance Bopoks, 1992.

Jordan, Stephanie and Dave Allen, eds. *Parallel Lines: Media Representations of Dance*. London: J. Libbey, 1993.

Kaye, Nick. *Postmodernism and Performance*. New York: St. Martin's Press, 1994.

Kirby, Michael. *The Art of Time: Essays on the Avant-Garde*. New York: E. P. Dutton & Co., 1969.

Kirstein, Lincoln. *By With To & From: A Lincoln Kirstein Reader;* edited by Nicholas Jenkins. New York: Farrar, Straus & Giroux, 1991.

Lange, Roderyk. *The Nature of Dance: An Anthropological Perspective*. New York: International Publications Service, 1975.

Levinson, André. *André Levinson on Dance: Writings from Paris in the Twenties,* ed. and with an introd. by Joan Acocella and Lynn Garafola. Hanover, N.H.: Wesleyan University Press, University Press of New England, 1991.

Louis, Murray. *Murray Louis on Dance*. Chicago: A Cappella Books, 1992.

McFee, Graham. *The Concept of Dance Education*. London, New York: Routledge, 1994.

————. *Understanding Dance*. London, New York: Routledge, 1992.

Martin, John Joseph, and Jack Anderson. *The Dance in Theory*, with a new introduction by Jack Anderson. Princeton, N.J.: Princeton Book Co., 1989.

Morris, Gay, ed. *Moving Words: Re-writing Dance*. London: New York: Routledge, 1996.

Murray, Timothy. *Drama Trauma: Specters of Race and Sexuality in Performance, Video, and Art*. London; New York: Routledge, 1997.

Nadel, Myron H., and C. N. Miller, ed. *The Dance Experience*. New York: Universe Books, 1978.

Nagrin, Daniel. *Dance and the Specific Image: Improvisation*. Pittsburgh: University of Pittsburgh Press, 1994.

Novack, Cynthia Jean. *Sharing the Dance: Contact Improvisation and American Culture*. New Directions in Anthropological Writing. Madison: University of Wisconsin Press, 1990.

Parker, Andrew, and Eve Kosofsky Sedgwick, eds. *Performativity and Performance*. New York : Routledge, 1995.

Phelan, Peggy. *The Politics of Performance*. London/New York: Routledge, 1993.

Pilates, Joseph H., and Miller, William John. *Return to Life through Contrology*. New York: J. J. Augustin Publisher, 1945.

Poirier, Richard. *Trying It Out: Literary and Other Performances*. New York: Farrar, Straus & Giroux, 1999.
> Includes an essay on George Balanchine and the New York City Ballet.

Reynolds, Dee. *Symbolist Aesthetics and Early Abstract Art: Sites of Imaginative Space*. Cambridge/New York: Cambridge University Press, 1995.

Royce, Anya Peterson. *Movement and Meaning: Creativity and Interpretation in Ballet and Mime*. Bloomington: Indiana University Press, 1984.

Schimmel, Paul. *Out of Actions: Between the Performance and the Object, 1949-1979*. Los Angeles: Museum of Contemporary Art, 1998.

Schneider, Rebecca. *The Explicit Body in Performance*. New York: Routledge, 1997.

Segal, Harold B. *Body Ascendant: Modernism and the Physical Imperative*. Baltimore: Johns Hopkins Press, 1998.

Shawn, Ted. *Every Little Movement: A Book about Francois Delsarte, the Man and His Philosophy, His Science and Applied Aesthetics, the*

Application of this Science to the Art of Dance, the Influence of Delsarte on American Dance. Brooklyn: Dance Horizons, 1963, rev. 1968

Sheets-Johnstone, Maxine. *The Phenomenology of Dance*. Madison: University of Wisconsin Press, 1966, 1980.

Shusterman, Richard. *Performing Live: Aesthetic Alternatives for the Ends of Art*. Ithaca, N.Y.: Cornell University Press, 2000.

Siegel, Marcia B. *The Tail of the Dragon: New Dance, 1976–1982*. Durham, N.C.: Duke University Press, 1991.

Sorell, Walter, ed. *The Dance Has Many Faces*. Rev. ed. New York: A Cappella Books, 1992.
    Earlier editions, 1951, 1966. Each edition has a changing selection of articles.

Souriau, Paul. *The Aesthetics of Movement*. Amherst: University of Massachusetts Press, 1983.

Sparshott, Francis Edward. *A Measured Pace: Toward a Philosophical Understanding of the Arts of Dance*. Toronto Studies in Philosophy. Toronto, Buffalo: University of Toronto Press, 1995.

Taplin, D. T., ed. *Dance Spectrum: Critical and Philosophical Enquiry*. Waterloo, Canada: University of Waterloo, 1982.

———, ed. *New Directions in Dance*. Oxford: Pergamon, 1979.

Taylor, Jim, and Ceci Taylor. *Psychology of Dance*. Champaign, Ill.: Human Kinetics, 1995.

Thomas, Helen. *Dance, Modernity, and Culture: Explorations in the Sociology of Dance*. London, New York: Routledge, 1995.

———. *Dance in the City*. New York: St. Martin's Press, 1997.

———, ed. *Dance, Gender, and Culture*. New York: St. Martin's Press, 1993.

Thompson, Robert Farris. *Flash of the Spirit: African and Afro-American Art and Philosophy*. New York: Random House, 1983.

Toepfer, Karl Eric. *Empire of Ecstasy: Nudity and Movement in German Body Culture, 1910–1935*. Berkeley: University of California Press, 1997.

Tomko, Linda J. *Dancing Class: Gender, Ethnicity, and Social Divides in American Dance, 1890–1920*. Bloomington: Indiana University Press, 1999.

Tufte, Edward R. *Envisioning Information*. Cheshire, Conn.: Graphics Press, 1990.

Wallace, Carol, et al. *Dance: A Very Social History*. New York: Metropolitan Museum of Art: Rizzoli, 1986.

Dance and Related Arts

This section contains sources on literature, visual art, design, music, photography, theater, costume, and film and their intersections with dance. See the Dance Theory section for sources related to the humanities and social sciences, such as philosophy, psychology, and other theoretical approaches to dance. Practical information about costuming for the stage and musical accompaniment are in the Dance Production and Administration section.

Print resources

Afternoon of a Faun: Mallarmé, Debussy, Nijinsky. New York: Vendome Press, distr. by Rizzoli, 1989.

Bidart, Frank. *In the Western Night: Collected Poems, 1965-90.* New York: Farrar Straus Giroux, 1990.
> Contains a 28-page poem "The War of Vaslav Nijinsky," and others inspired by ballet.

Brissendon, Alan. *Shakespeare and the Dance.* London: Macmillan, 1981.

Cage, John. *Silence: Lectures and Writings by John Cage.* 1961. Hanover, N.H.: Wesleyan University Press.

Deren, Maya. *A Documentary Biography and Collected Works.* Veve Clark, ed. New York: Anthology Film Archives/Film Culture, 1984.
> Working process of a pioneer artist in cinedance and in the Haitian rituals of voudoun.

Diller, Elizabeth and Ricardo Scofidio. *Flesh: Architectural Probes.* Essay by Georges Teyssot. New York: Princeton Architectural Press, 1994.

Fehl, Fred. *Fred Fehl at New York City Ballet.* New York: Dance Research Foundation, 1992. Performance photographs 1948 to ca. 1980.

Gaddis, Eugene R. *Magician of the Modern: Chick Austin.* New York: Alfred A. Knopf, 2000.
> As a museum curator, Austin's artistic circle encompassed Gertrude Stein, Virgil Thompson, Lincoln Kirstein, George Balanchine, Philip Johnson, and American folk artists.

Goellner, Ellen W., and Jacqueline Shea Murphy, eds. *Bodies of the Text: Dance as Theory, Literature as Dance.* New Brunswick, N.J.: Rutgers University Press, 1995.

Green, Jonathan, ed. *Continuous Replay: The Photographs of Arnie Zane.* Cambridge: M.I.T. Press, 1999.

Records the early choreographic work of Bill T. Jones.

Greenfield, Lois. *Breaking Bounds: The Dance Photography of Lois Greenfield.* With text by William A. Ewing. San Francisco: Chronicle Books, 1992.

Haring, Keith. *Dance.* Boston: Bullfinch Press, 1999.

A contemporary painter records his inspirations in hip-hop dancing.

Hoffman, Katherine. *Georgia O'Keefe: A Celebration of Music and Dance.* New York: George Braziller, 1997.

Hollander, Anne. *Sex and Suits: The Evolution of Modern Dress.* New York: Knopf, 1994.

Holmberg, Arthur. *The Theatre of Robert Wilson.* Cambridge, New York: Cambridge University Press, 1996.

Jordan, Stephanie and Dave Allen. *Parallel Lines: Media Representations of Dance.* London: J. Libbey, 1993.

Kendall, Richard. *Degas Dancers.* New York: Universe/Vendome, 1996.

Kirstein, Lincoln. *Quarry: A Collection in Lieu of Memoirs.* Pasadena, Calif.: Twelvetrees Press, 1986.

Leong, Roger. *From Russia with Love: Costumes for the Ballets Russes 1909-1933.* Canberra: National Gallery of Australia, 1998.

Moses, Lester George. *Wild West Shows and the Images of American Indians.* Albuquerque: University of New Mexico Press, 1996.

Mueller, John. *Astaire Dancing: The Musical Films.* New York: Alfred A. Knopf, 1985.

Pozharskaya, Militsa, and Tatiana Volodina, eds. *The Art of the Ballets Russes: The Russian Seasons in Paris 1909-1929.* London: Aurumn Press, 1990.

Rinehart, Robert E. *Players All: Performances in Contemporary Sport.* Bloomington: Indiana University Press, 1998.

Schouvaloff, Alexander. *The Art of the Ballets Russes: The Serge Lifar Collection of Theater Designs, Costumes and Paintings at the Wadsworth Atheneum.* New Haven: Yale University Press and the Wadsworth Atheneum, 1997.

Searle, Humphrey. *Ballet Music: An Introduction.* 2nd. ed. New York: Dover Publications, Inc., 1973.

———. *Léon Bakst: The Theatre Art*. London: Sotheby's Publications and Philip Wilson Publishers, 1991.

Sharma, Sanjoy P., John Hutnyk, and Ashwani Sharma. *Dis-Orienting Rhythms: The Politics of New Asian Dance Music*. London: Zed Books, distr. St. Martin's Press, 1996.

Solomon, Deborah. *Utopia Parkway: The Life and Work of Joseph Cornell*. New York: Farrar, Straus & Giroux, 1997.

Teck, Katherine. *Ear Training for the Body: A Dancer's Guide to Music*. Hightstown, N.J.: Princeton Books, 1994.

———. *Music for the Dance: Reflections on a Collaborative Art*. Westport, Conn.: Greenwood Publishing Group, 1989.

Volkov, Solomon. *Balanchine's Tchaikovsky: Interviews with George Balanchine*. NY: Simon and Schuster, 1985.

Nonprint resources

The Collaborators: Cage, Cunningham, Rauschenberg, prod. Angela Davis, 55 min., distr. Merce Cunningham Dance Foundation, 1987. Videocassette.

Maya Deren: Experimental Films, prod. Alexander Hackenschmied, dir. Maya Deren, 76 min., distr. Mystic Fire Video, Women Make Movies, 1943-1959. Videocassette.

　　　Compilation of short films including *Meshes of the Afternoon, Ritual in Transfigured Time*, and *Meditation on Violence*.

Merce by Merce by Paik. 30 min., prod. WNET-TV, distr. Merce Cunningham Dance Foundation; New York: Electronic Arts Intermix, 1978. Videocassette.

　　　Collaboration between Merce Cunningham, Charles Atlas, Nam June Paik, and Shigeko Kubota.

Selection criteria for this section are based on broad subject areas including dance education, dance pedagogy, movement education, and aesthetic education. Dance education aims to develop skills in self-expression and abstraction through movement. Dance education and dance pedagogy share a focus on the body and its movement potential. Movement education provides experiences about the movement of the body in space with the use of dynamics. Models of this derive from Rudolf Laban and Margaret H'Doubler. Aesthetic education seeks to define values and stylistic preferences within the art form of dance. Some works on the philosophy of education that inform dance and arts education have been included in this section. Textbooks, teaching manuals, and "how-to" handbooks have not been included. Works related to movement approaches and techniques that support and enhance general health and well being appear in this section as well as the Dance Medicine and Science, Dance Therapy, and Somatic Studies sections. See also the section on Dance Theory.

Print resources

Allcock, Rita. *Dance in Education.* London: Dance Books, 1980.

Benzwie, T. *More Moving Experiences: Connecting Arts, Feelings and Imagination (Grades K-12).* Tucson: Ariz.: Zephyr Press, 1996.

———. *A Moving Experience: Dance for Lovers of Children and the Child Within.* Tucson, Ariz.: Zephyr Press, 1987.

Boas, Franziska. *The Function of Dance in Human Society,* New York: The Boas School, 1944.

Brinson, Peter. *Dance Education and Training in Britain.* London: Calouste Gulbenkian Foundation, 1994.

———. *Dance as Education: Towards a National Dance Culture.* London: New York: Falmer, 1991.

Chapman, Sarah. *Movement Education in the United States.* Philadelphia: Movement Education Publications, 1974.

Colby, Gertrude. *Natural Rhythms and Dance.* New York: A. S. Barnes & Co., 1922.

Dance History: An Introduction. Janet Adshead-Lansdale and June Lawson, eds. 2nd ed. London; New York: Routledge, 1994.

Davies, Ann. *Bodywork: Primary Children, Dance and Gymnastics.* Cheltenham: S. Thornes, 1995.

Dewey, John. *Art as Experience.* New York: Minton, Balch & Co., 1934.

Dunning, Jennifer. *"But First A School": The First Fifty Years of the School of American Ballet.* New York: Viking, 1985.

Eddy, M. *The Role of Physical Activity in Educational Violence Prevention Programs for Youth.* Ph.D. diss., Teachers College, Columbia University, 1998.

Evans, Judy. *Inspirations for Dance and Movement.* Leamington Spa: Scholastic, 1994.

Forti, Simone. *Handbook in Motion.* New York: New York University Press, 1974.

Foster, John. *The Influence of Rudolph Laban.* London: Lepus Books, 1977.

Fowler, Charles. *Dance as Education.* Washington, D.C.: National Dance Association, 1977.

Gardner, Harold. *Frames of Mind: The Theory of Multiple Intelligences.* New York: Basic Books, 1993.

Greene, Maxine. *Landscapes of Learning.* New York: Teachers College Press, 1978.

Guest, Ann Hutchinson. *Your Move: a New Approach to the Study of Movement and Dance.* Gordon & Breach, 1983.

Hanna, Judith Lynne. *Partnering Dance and Education: Intelligent Moves for Changing Times.* Champaign, Ill.: Human Kinetics, 1999.

Hawkins, Alma. *Creating Through Dance,* rev. ed. Pennington, N.J.: Princeton Book Co./Dance Horizons, 1988.

———. *Modern Dance in Higher Education.* New York: Teachers College Press, 1954.

H'Doubler, Margaret N. *The Dance and Its Place in Education.* New York: Harcourt, Brace, & Co., 1925.

———. *Dance: A Creative Art Experience,* 2nd. ed. Madison: University of Wisconsin Press, 1957.

———. *The Dance.* New York: Harcourt, Brace & Co., 1925.

Jaques-Dalcroze, Emile. Trans. Harold F. Rubenstein. *Rhythm, Music and Education* (Reprint). New York: Arno Press, 1976.

———. *The Eurhythmics of Jaques-Dalcroze.* Boston: Small, Maynard & Co., 1918.

Kaagan, Stephen. *Aesthetic Persuasion: Pressing the Cause of Arts Education in American Schools.* Los Angeles, Calif.: Getty Center for Education in the Arts, 1990.

King, Bruce. *Creative Dance; Experience for Learning.* Bozeman: Montana State University, 1968.

Kraus, Richard G., Sarah Chapman Hilsendager, and Brenda Dixon Gottschild. *History of the Dance in Art and Education,* 3rd ed. Englewood Cliffs, N.J.: Prentice-Hall, 1991.

Laban, Rudolf. *Rudolf Laban Speaks about Movement and Dance: Lectures and Articles.* Addlestone, Surrey: Laban Art of Movement Centre. 1971.

———. *Modern Educational Dance,* 3rd ed., Lisa Ullmann, ed., London: MacDonald & Evans, 1975.

———. *A Life for Dance: Reminiscences.* Trans. Lisa Ullmann. London: Macdonald & Evans, 1975.

———. *The Language of Movement.* Boston: Plays, Inc., 1974.

———. *The Mastery of Movement,* 3rd ed. London: MacDonald & Evans, 1971.

Lavender, Larry. *Dancers Talking Dance: Critical Evaluation in the Choreography Class.* Champaign, Ill.: Human Kinetics, 1996.

Lee, Alison. *A Handbook of Creative Dance and Drama.* Portsmouth, N.H.: Heinemann, 1991.

Lerman, Liz. *Teaching Dance to Senior Adults.* Springfield, Ill.: Thomas Books, 1984.

Marks, Joseph E. *America Learns to Dance: A Historical Study of Dance Education in America Before 1900.* New York: Dance Horizons, 1976.

McFee, Graham. *The Concept of Dance Education.* London & New York: Routledge, 1994.

Mettler, Barbara. *Dance as an Element of Life.* Tucson, Ariz.: Mettler Studios, 1985.

Minton, Sandra Cerny. *Dance Education Research and Supplementary Articles.* Bethesda, Md.: National Dance Education Organization, 1999.

Morrison, Jeffrey. *Winckelman and the Notion of Aesthetic Education.* Oxford: Clarendon Press, 1996.

Murray, Ruth L. *Dance in Elementary Education.* New York: Harper & Row, 1975.

Preston-Dunlap, Valerie. *Handbook for Modern Educational Dance.* Boston, Mass.: Plays, Inc., 1980.

————. *Practical Kinetography Laban*. London: MacDonald & Evans, 1969.

Rath, Emil. *Aesthetic Dancing*. New York: A. S. Barnes, 1928.

Redfern, Betty. *Questions in Aesthetic Education*. London & Boston: Allen & Unwin, 1986.

Rogers, Frederick. *Dance: A Basic Educational Technique* (reprint). New York: Dance Horizons, 1980.

Royal Academy of Dancing. *Ballet in Education*. London: 1954.

Russell, Joan. *Modern Dance in Education*. London: MacDonald & Evans, 1958.

————. *Creative Dance in the Primary School*. London: MacDonald & Evans, 1992.

Ruyter, Nancy Lee Chalfa. *Reformers and Visionaries: The Americanization of the Art of Dance*. New York: Dance Horizons, 1979.

Schlaich, Joan, and Betty DuPont. *The Art of Teaching Dance Technique*. Reston, Va.: National Dance Association, 1993.

Shapiro, Sherry. *Pedagogy and the Politics of the Body: A Critical Praxis*. New York: Garland Publishers, 1999.

————. *Dance, Power, and Difference: Critical and Feminist Perspectives on Dance Education*. Champaign, Ill.: Human Kinetics, 1998.

Sienkiewicz, Carol L. *From Theory to Practice: The Development of the Lincoln Center Institute's Model of Aesthetic Education*, 1986.

Smith, Jacqueline. *Dance Composition: A Practical Guide for Teachers*. London: Lepus Books, 1976.

Smith-Autard, Jacqueline M. *The Art of Dance in Education*. London: Black, 1994.

Stinson, Susan. *Dance for Young Children: Finding the Magic in Movement*. Reston, Va.: AAHPERD, 1988.

Thomas, Jerry. *Introduction to Research in Health, Physical Education, Recreation and Dance*. Champaign, Ill.: Human Kinetics, 1985.

Varley, G. *To Be a Dancer: Canada's National Ballet School*. Toronto: Peter Martins Associates, 1971.

Nonprint resources

JVC Video Anthology of World Music and Dance. Editor, Fujii Tomoaki; assistant editors, Omori Yasuhiro, Sakurai Tetsuo; in collaboration with the National Museum of Ethnology (Osaka.)

Standards Reference Master. (CD Rom). Phoenix, Ariz.: Teachmaster Technologies, 1999.

Dance Ethnology and the Anthropology of Dance

Recent trends in dance studies suggest that the terms "Western dance" and "non-Western dance" perpetuate false dichotomies and that a focus on who studies the dances, and their points of view, might be more appropriate. Cultural forms of human bodies in time and space are often glossed as "dance," but the word itself carries with it preconceptions. Dance is a phenomenon that includes in addition to what we see and hear the "invisible" underlying system and the socio-political context. Analyses from anthropoogical points of view encompass all structured movement systems, including those associated with religious and secular ritual, ceremony, entertainment, martial arts, sign languages, sports and games. The focus of dance ethnologists, in contrast, is on dance content, and the study of cultural context aims at illuminating the dance. In these studies, the social relationships of the people dancing are often backgrounded while the dance itself and its changes over time are foregrounded. Included in this section are sources that reflect this definition, and which include ethnographic and anthropological studies as well as philosophical treatises on the analysis of human movement. Extensive source material is available in the periodical literature. See also the sections on Dance Theory, Dance Education, and the individual sections under Dance Forms, Styles and Traditions.

Print resources

Azzi, Maria Susana. *Antropologia del Tango, los Protagonistas.* Buenos Aires: Ediciones Olavarria, 1991.

Boas, Franziska. *The Function of Dance in Human Society.* New York: The Boas School, 1944; 2d ed., Brooklyn, N.Y.: Dance Horizons, 1972.

Buckland, Theresa, ed. *Dance in the Field. Theory, Methods and Issues in Dance Ethnography.* London: Macmillan, 1999.

Comstock, Tamara, ed. *New Dimensions in Dance Research: Anthropology and Dance—The American Indian.* CORD Research Annual VI. New York: Committee on Research in Dance, 1974.

Cowan, Jane K. *Dance and the Body Politic in Northern Greece.* Princeton: Princeton University Press, 1990.

Drewal. M. T. *Yoruba Ritual: Performers, Play, Agency*. Bloomington: University of Indiana Press, 1992.

Farnell, Brenda M. *Plains Indian Sign-talk and the Embodiment of Action*. Austin: University of Texas Press, 1994.

———, ed. *Human Action Signs in Cultural Context. The Visible and the Invisible in Movement and Dance*. Metuchen, N.J., Scarecrow Press, 1995.

Foster, Susan Leigh. *Reading Dancing. Bodies and Subjects in Contemporary American Dance*. Berkeley: University of California Press, 1986.

Giurchescu, Anca with Sunni Bloland. *Romanian Traditional Dance: A Contextual and Structural Approach*. Mill Valley, Calif.: Wild Flower Press, 1995.

Hanna, Judith Lynne. *To Dance is Human: A Theory of Nonverbal Communication*. Austin: University of Texas Press, 1979.

———. *Dance, Sex and Gender*. Chicago: University of Chicago Press, 1988.

Jones, Betty True, ed. *Dance as Cultural Heritage*. Dance Research Annual, 14–15. 2 vols. NY: Congress On Research in Dance, 1983–1985.

Kaeppler, Adrienne Lois. *Hula Pahu Hawaiian Drum Dances*. Volume 1. *Ha'a and Hula Pahu: Sacred Movements*. Honolulu: Bishop Museum, 1993.

———. *Poetry in Motion: Studies of Tongan Dance*. Tonga: Vava'u Press, 1993.

———. *Polynesian Dance: With a Selection for Contemporary Performances*. Honolulu: Alpha Delta Kappa, 1983.
    Privately printed by Alpha Delta Kappa-Hawai'i. Includes 8 dance songs from 5 island areas with instructions for dancing.

Keali'inohomoku, Joann W. *Theories and Methods for an Anthropological Study of Dance*. Ph.D. diss., University of Indiana, 1976.

Kligman, Gail. *Calus: Symbolic Transformation in Romanian Ritual*. Foreword by Mircea Eliade. Chicago: University of Chicago Press, 1981.

Kurath, Gertrude Prokosch and Antonio García. *Music and Dance of the Tewa Pueblos*. Santa Fe, N.M.: Museum of New Mexico Press, 1970.

Lewis, John Lowell. *Ring of Liberation: Deceptive Discourse in Brazilian Capoeira*. University of Chicago Press, 1992.

Loken-Kim, Christine. *Release from Bitterness: Korean Dancer as Korean Woman*. Ph.D. diss., Chapel Hill: University of North Carolina, 1989.

Lomax, Alan. *Folk Song Style and Culture*. Washington, D.C.: American Association for the Advancement of Science, 1968.

Loutzaki, Irene. *Dance As A Cultural Message. A Study of Dance Style among the Greek Refugees from Northern Thrace*. Ph.D. diss., Belfast, Ireland: The Queen's University of Belfast, 1989.

Malinowski, Bronislaw. *Argonauts of the Western Pacific*. New York: E.P. Dutton and Co., 1922.

Ness, Sally Ann. *Body, Movement, and Culture: Kinesthetic and Visual Symbolism in a Philippine Community*. Philadelphia:University of Pennsylvania Press, 1992.

Novack, Cynthia Jean. *Sharing the Dance: Contact Improvisation and American Culture*. New Directions in Anthropological Writing. Madison: University of Wisconsin Press, 1990.

Quigley, Colin. *Close to the Floor: Folk Dance in Newfoundland*. St. John's: Memorial University of Newfoundland, Folklore Department, 1985.

Royce, Anya Peterson. *The Anthropology of Dance*. Bloomington: University of Indiana Press, 1977.

Sachs, Curt. *World History of the Dance*. Trans. Bessie Schöenberg. New York: W.W. Norton, 1937.

Schieffelin, Edward L. *The Sorrow of the Lonely and the Burning of the Dancers*. New York: St. Martin's Press, 1976.

Solomon, Ruth, and John Solomon, eds. *East Meets West in Dance: Voices in the Cross-Cultural Dialogue*. Choreography and Dance Studies, v. 9. Chur, Switzerland: Harwood Academic Publishers, 1995.
Collection of essays on the issues involved in transplanting Western dance to the east and guidance for those who wish to participate in the endeavor.

Spencer, Paul, ed. *Society and the Dance. The Social Anthropology of Process and Performance*. Cambridge University Press, 1985.

Sweet, Jill D. *Dances of the Tewa Pueblo Indians: Expressions of New Life*. Santa Fe, N.M.: School of American Research Press, 1985.

Torp, Lisbet. *Chain and Round Dance Patterns. A Method for Structural Analysis and Its Application to European Material.* Copenhagen, Denmark: Museum Tusculanum Press, 1990.

Van Zile, Judy. *The Japanese Bon Dance in Hawaii.* Hawaii: Press Pacifica, 1982.

Williams, Drid. *Anthropology and Human Movement.* Lanham, Md.; Scarecrow Press, 1997– .

> *Vol. 1, Anthropology and Human Movement: The Study of Dances* (1997).
>
> *Vol. 2, Anthropology and Human Movement: Searching For Origins* (2000).

———. *Ten Lectures on Theories of the Dance.* Metuchen, N.J.: Scarecrow Press, 1991.

Nonprint resources

JVC Video Anthology of World Music and Dance. Editor, Fujii Tomoaki; assistant editors, Omori Yasuhiro, Sakurai Tetsuo; in collaboration with the National Museum of Ethnology (Osaka.)

Dance Science and Medicine

The area of dance medicine and science draws from the combined fields of anatomy and physiology, kinesiology, biomechanics, general medicine, sports medicine and surgery, physical therapy, dance education, psychology, and nutrition and diet. This arena includes the identification, treatment, rehabilitation, and prevention of illnesses and injuries. The application of scientific research encompasses dance training and performance. Whereas the field of dance science is influenced by somatic studies, in this core collection bibliography somatic studies is treated in a discreet section. Standard works, such as textbooks and manuals on anatomy, kinesiology, and physiology are not included. Works related to movement approaches and techniques that support and enhance general health and well being appear in this section as well as the Dance Education, Dance Therapy, and Somatic Studies sections. See also the section on Dance Theory.

Print resources

Abstracts of the Seventh Annual Symposium on Medical Problems of Musicians and Dancers. Snowmass, Colo.: 1989.

Arnheim, Daniel D. *Dance Injuries: Their Prevention and Cure.* Princeton, N.J.: Princeton Book Company, Publishers, 1986.

Barham, Jerry N. *Mechanical Kinesiology.* St. Louis, Mo.: C. V. Mosby Company, 1978.

Butler, Brian H. *Introduction to Kinesiology: Natural Way to "Balanced Health" and "Well Being".* 2d ed. Surbiton, Surrey: T.A.S.K. Books, 1995.

Calais-Germain, Blandine. *Anatomy of Movement.* Seattle, Wash.: Eastland Press, Inc., 1993.

Clarkson, Priscilla M., and Margaret Skrinar. *Science of Dance Training.* Champaign, Ill.: Human Kinetics Books, 1988.

Cooper, John M., Adrian, Marlene, and Glassow, Ruth B. *Kinesiology.* 5th ed. St. Louis, Mo.: C.V. Mosby Company, 1982.

Dowd, Irene. *Taking Root to Fly: Articles on Functional Anatomy.* Northhampton, Mass.: Contact Edition, 1998.

Fitt, Chmelar, and Sally Sevey Fitt. *Diet: A Complete Guide to Nutrition and Weight Control.* Princeton, N.J.: Princeton Book Company, 1990.

Fitt, Sally Sevey. *Dance Kinesiology.* 2d ed. New York: Schirmer Books, 1996.

Gelabert, Raol. *Anatomy for Dancers, v. I & II.* New York: Dance Magazine, 1964.

————. *Anatomy for the Dancer, with Exercises to Improve Technique and Prevent Injuries, as told to William Como.* New York, Danad Publishing Company, 1964.

Holdway, Ann. *Kinesiology: Muscle Testing and Energy Balancing for Health and Well Being.* Shaftsbury, Dorset: Element Books Limited, 1996.

Howse, Justin, and Hancock, Shirley. *Dance Technique and Injury Prevention.* London: A & C Black (Publishers) Ltd., 1988.

Jensen, Clayne R., Gordon W. Schultz, and Blauer L. Bangerter. *Applied Kinesiology and Biomechanics.* 3rd ed. New York: McGraw-Hill Book Company, 1983.

Knott, Margaret, and Dorothy Voss. *Proprioceptive Neuromuscular Facilitation.* New York: Harper & Row, 1956.

Kopciks, V., and A. Subnikovs. *Symmetry in Science and Art.* Moscow: Nauka, 1972.

Laws, Kenneth, and Cynthia Harvey. *Physics, Dance, and the Pas de Deux.* New York: Schirmer Books, 1994.

Laws, Kenneth. *The Physics of Dance.* New York: Schirmer Books, 1984.

Luttgens, Kathryn, and Katherine F. Wells. *Kinesiology: Scientific Basis of Human Motion.* 7th ed. Philadelphia: Saunders College Publishing, 1982.

Lycholat, Tony. *The Complete Book of Stretching.* Bristol, England: The Crowood Press, 1996.

Olsen, Andrea. *Body Stories: a Guide to Experimental Anatomy.* Barrytown, N.Y.: Station Hill Press, 1991.

Paskevska, Anna. *Both Sides of the Mirror: The Science and Art of Ballet.* Princeton, N.J.: Princeton Book Company, 1992.

Pierce, Alexandra, and Roger Pierce. *Expressive Movement: Posture and Action in Daily Life, Sports, and the Performing Arts.* New York, London: Plenium Press, c. 1989.

Ryan, Allan J., and Robert E. Stephens, editors. *Dance Medicine: A Comprehensive Guide.* Chicago: Pluribus Press, Inc., 1987.

————. *The Healthy Dancer: Dance Medicine for Dancers.* Princeton, N.J.: Princeton Book Company, 1987.

Sammarco, James. *Clinics in Sports Medicine: Injuries to Dancers.* Philadelphia: W. B. Saunders, 1983.

Sataloff, Robert Thayer, Alice G. Brandfonbrener, and Richard J. Lederman, eds. *Textbook of Performing Arts Medicine.* New York: Raven Press, 1991.

Shell, Caroline G. ed. *The Dancer as Athlete.* The 1984 Olympic Scientific Congress Proceedings, vol. 8. Champaign, Ill.: Human Kinetics Publishers, Inc., 1986.

Solomon, Ruth, and John Solomon, compilers. *Dance Medicine & Science Bibliography.* Andover, N.J.: Michael Ryan Publishers, 1996.

Solomon, Ruth, Sandra Cerny Minton, and John Solomon. *Preventing Dance Injuries: An Interdisciplinary Perspective.* Reston, Va.: NDA/AAHPERD, 1990.

Soviet-American Dance Medicine: Proceedings of the 1990 Glasnost Dance Medicine Conference and Workshops. Lyle Micheli, Ruth Solomon, and John Solomon, eds. Reston, Va.: AAPHERD, 1991.

Sparger, Celia. *Ballet Physique: with Notes on Stresses and Injuries.* London: Adam and Charles Black, 1958.

———. *Anatomy and Ballet.* London: Adam and Charles Black, 1970.

Spilken, Terry L., M.D. *The Dancer's Foot Book: a Complete Guide to Footcare and Health for People Who Dance.* Pennington, N.J.: Princeton Book Co., 1990.

Storojeff, Igor. *A Scientific Approach to Teaching Ballet.* Hypoluxo, Fla.: Er-Mur, Inc., 1976.

Thomasen, Eivind, and Rachel-Anne Rist. *Anatomy and Kinesiology for Ballet Teachers.* London: Dance Books, 1996.

Vincent, L. M. *The Dancer's Book of Health.* New York: Andrews & McNeel, 1978.

Watkins, Andrea, and Priscilla M. Clarkson. *Dancing Longer, Dancing Stronger: a Dancer's Guide to Improving Technique and Preventing Injury.* Princeton, N.J.: Princeton Book Company, 1990.

Wessel, Janet, and Christine Macintyre. *Body Contouring and Conditioning Through Movement.* Boston: Allen & Bacon, 1970.

Wright, Stuart. *Dancer's Guide to Injuries of the Lower Extremity.* New York: Cornwall Books, 1985.

DANCE THERAPY

Dance therapy seeks to bring change in behavior, communication, self-concepts, body image, and personal expression through a therapeutic process that is primarily psychodynamic in nature. Because dance therapy treats those diagnosed with mental and emotional disorders, dance therapists are often trained in psychology, counseling, and group dynamics. Works related to movement approaches and techniques that support and enhance general health and well being appear in this section as well as the Dance Education, Dance Medicine and Science, and Somatic Studies sections. See also the section on Dance Theory.

Print resources

Bartenieff, Irmgard, and Martha Ann Davis. *Effort-Shape Analysis of Movement: The Unity of Expression and Function.* New York: Albert Einstein College of Medicine, Yeshiva University, 1965.

Bartenieff, Irmgard, Martha Ann Davis, and Forrestine Paulay. *Four Adaptations of Effort Theory in Research and Teaching.* New York: Dance Notation Bureau, Inc., 1973.

Bartenieff, Irmgard, and Dori Lewis. *Body Movement: Coping with the Environment.* New York: Gordon and Breach Science Publishers, 1980.

Bartenieff, Irmgard, and Irma Otte-Betz. *Elementary Studies in Laban's Dance Script.* New York, 1937.

Berardi, Gigi. *Finding Balance: Fitness and Training for a Lifetime in Dance.* Princeton, N.J.: Princeton Book Company, 1991.

Bernstein, Penny Lewis. *Dance/Movement Therapy.* Dubuque, Iowa: Kendall/Hunt, 1979.

———. *Eight Theoretical Approaches in Dance Movement Therapy.* Dubuque, Iowa: Kendall-Hunt Publishing Co., 1979.

Caplow-Lindner, Erna. *Theraputic Dance Movement: Expressive Activities for Older Adults.* New York: Human Sciences Press, 1979.

Chace, Marian, *Marian Chace: Her Papers.* Harris Chaiklin, ed. Kensington Md: American Dance Therapy Association, 1975.

Chodorow, Joan. *Dance Therapy and Depth Psychology: The Moving Imagination.* London & New York: Routledge, 1991.

Corbin, David E., and Josie Metal-Corbin. *Reach for It!: A Handbook of Exercise and Dance Activities for Older Adults.* Dubuque, Iowa: Eddie Bowers Pub. Co., 1983.

Costonis, Maureen Needham, ed. *Therapy in Motion.* Urbana, IL: University of Illinois Press, 1978.

Dance for the Handicapped. Reston, Va.: National Dance Association, 1980.

Drake, Jonathan. *The Alexander Technique in Everyday Life.* London: Thorsons, 1996.

Earl, William L. *A Dancer Takes Flight: Psychological Concerns in the Development the American Male Dance.* Lanham, Md.: University Press of America, 1988.

Espenak, Lilijan. *Dance Therapy: Theory and Application.* Springfield, Ill.: Charles C. Thomas, 1981.

Evan, Blanche. *The Child's World: Its Relation to Dance Pedagogy.* New York: St. Marks Editions, 1964.

Exiner, Johanna et al. *Dance Therapy Redefined: A Body Approach to Therapeutic Dance.* Springfield, Ill.: Charles C. Thomas, 1994.

Featherstone, D.F. *Dancing Without Anger,* 2nd ed. New York: A.S. Barnes, 1977.

Feldenkrais, Moshe. *Body and Mature Behavior.* New York: International Universities Press, 1949.

———. *Awareness through Movement: Health Exercises for Personal Growth.* New York: Harper & Row, 1972.

———. *The Illusive Obvious.* Cupertino, Calif.: META Publications, 1981.

Fisher, Pauline P. *Creative Movement for Older Adults; Exercises for the Fit to Frail.* New York: Human Sciences Press, Inc., 1989.

Franklin, Eric N. *Dynamic Alignment Through Imagery.* Champaign, Ill.: Human Kinetics, 1996.

Friedman, Philip, and Gail Eisen. *The Pilates Method of Physical and Mental Conditioning.* Garden City, N.Y.: Doubleday & Company, 1980.

Halprin, Anna. *Moving Toward Life: Five Decades of Transformational Dance.* Hanover & London: Wesleyan University Press, 1995.

Hanna, Judith Lynne. *Dance and Stress: Resistance, Reduction, and Euphoria.* Stress in Modern Society, no. 13. New York: AMS Press, Inc., 1988.

Levy, Fran J., Judith Pines Fried, and Fern Leventhal, eds. *Dance and Other Expressive Art Therapies: When Words are not Enough*. New York: Routledge, 1995.

Levy, Fran J. *Dance/Movement Therapy: A Healing Art*. rev. ed. Reston, Va.: National Dance Association, an association of the American Alliance for Health, Physical Education, Recreation and Dance, 1992.

Morgan, Doug. *T.T.T.: an Introduction to Trance Dancing*. Lantzville, B. C.: Ship Cottage Press, 1988.

Payne, Helen. *Creative Movement & Dance in Groupwork*. Bicester, Oxon: Winslow Press, 1992.

————, ed. *Dance Movement Therapy: Theory and Practice*. London & New York: Tavistock/Routledge, 1992.

Rosen, Elizabeth. *Dance in Psychotherapy*. New York: Dance Horizons Republication, 1974.

Salkin, Jeri. *Body Ego Technique: An Educational and Therapeutic Approach to Body Image and Self-Identity*. Springfield, Ill.: Charles C Thomas, Publisher, 1973.

Sandel, Susan L., Sharon Chaiklin, and Ann Lohn, eds. *Foundations of Dance/Movement Therapy: The Life and Work of Marian Chace*. Columbus Md.: Marion Chace Memorial Fund of the American Dance Therapy Association, 1993.

Shoop, Trudy. *Won't You Join in the Dance? A Dancer's Essay into the Treatment of Psychosis*. Palo Alto, Calif.: National Press Books, 1974.

Siegel, Elaine V. *Dance-Movement Therapy: The Mirror of Ourselves: A Psychoanalytic Approach*. NY: Human Sciences Press, 1984.

Stanton-Jones, Kristina. *An Introduction to Dance Movement Therapy in Psychiatry*. London; New York: Tavistock/Routledge, 1992.

Sweigard, Lulu E. *Human Movement Potential: Its Ideokinetic Facilitation*. New York: Harper & Row, Publishers, Inc., 1974.

Wethered, Audrey G. *Movement and Drama in Therapy: A Holistic Approach*. 2^d ed. London; Philadelphia: Jessica Kingsley Publishers, 1993.

Nonprint resources

Dancing from the Inside Out. In Sight Productions. El Cerrito, Calif.: Dancing Video, 1993. 28 min.

> Dancers in wheelchairs who are members of the Axis Dance Company discuss their disabilities and what dance means to them.

SOMATIC STUDIES

Somatic studies include the combined work of numerous artists, educators, and scientists influenced by non-western traditions or non-Cartesian models of the exploration of human experience. The discipline of somatic studies refers to the investigation of the whole person inclusive of his/her associated physical and emotional needs. Somatic studies in dance are best represented through those movement disciplines that teach movement re-education, and re-patterning, emphasizing active and visual movement experiences as well as a variety of hands-on techniques. Somatic studies are otherwise referred to as body therapy, body/mind discipline, somatic movement therapy, or holistic bodywork. Included are original works and texts by the innovators and initiators of the somatic discipline, adaptations of those theorists as applied to movement expression and dance performance, and deeper theoretical discussions of developmental issues. Works related to movement approaches and techniques that support and enhance general health and well being appear in this section as well as the Dance Education, Dance Medicine and Science, and Dance Therapy sections. See also the section on Dance Theory.

Print resources

Alcantara, Pedro De. *Indirect Procedures: A Musician's Guide to the Alexander Technique.* New York: Oxford University Press, 1997.

Alexander, F.M. *Alexander Technique: The Essential Writings of F.M. Alexander: Constructive Conscious Control [Abridged.]* London: Thames and Hudson, 1990.

Bainbridge-Cohen, Bonnie. *Sensing, Feeling, & Action.* Northampton, Mass.: Contact Editions, 1993.

Bainbridge-Cohen, Bonnie, and Margaret Mills. *Developmental Movement Therapy.* Northampton, Mass.: The School for Body-Mind Centering, 1986.

Bartenieff, Irmgard. *Body Movement: Coping with the Environment.* New York: Gordon and Breach Science Publishers, 1980.

Bruser, Madeline. *The Art of Practicing: A Guide to Making Music from the Heart.* New York: Bell Tower, 1997.

Calais-Germain, Blandine. *Anatomy of Movement.* Seattle, Wash.: Eastland Press, 1993.

Cranz, Galen. *The Chair: Rethinking Culture, Body, and Design.* New York: W.W. Norton & Company, 1998.

Cole, Jonathan. *About Face.* Cambridge, Mass.: MIT Press, 1998.

Damasio, Antonio. *Descartes' Error: Emotion, Reason and the Human Brain.* New York: G.P. Putnam, 1994.

———. *The Feeling of What Happens: Body and Emotion in the Making of Consciousness.* New York: Harcourt Brace, 1999.

Dowd, Irene. *Taking Root to Fly: Articles on Functional Anatomy.* Northhampton, Mass.: Contact Edition, 1998.

Drake, Jonathon. *The Alexander Technique in Everyday Life.* London: Thorsons, 1996.

Feldenkrais, Moshe. *Body Awareness as Healing Therapy: The Case of Nora.* Berkeley, Calif.: Somatic Resources, 1977.

———. *Awareness Through Movement: Health Exercises for Personal Growth.* New York: Harper and Row, 1997

———. *Master Moves.* Capitola, Calif.: Meta Publications, 1985.

———. *The Potent Self: A Guide to Spontaneity.* San Francisco: Harper San Francisco, 1992.

———. *Body and Mature Behavior.* New York: International Universities Press, 1949.

Fitt, Sally Sevey. *Dance Kinesiology.* 2d ed. New York: Schirmer Books, 1996.

Franklin, Eric N. *Dynamic Alignment through Imagery.* Champaign, Ill.: Human Kinetics, 1996.

Friedman, Philip, and Gail Eisen. *The Pilates Method of Physical and Mental Conditioning.* Garden City, N.Y.: Doubleday & Company, 1980.

Goldman, Ellen. *As Others See Us: Body Movement and the Art of Successful Communication.* New York: Gordon and Breach, 1994.

Gomez, Ninoska. *Movement, Body and Awareness: Exploring Somatic Processes,* Montreal: N. Gomez, 1988.

Greene, Maxine. *Releasing the Imagination: Essays on Education, the Arts, and Social Change.* San Francisco: Jossey-Bass Publishers, 1995.

Halprin, Anna. *Moving Toward Life: Five Decades of Transformational Dance.* Hanover, London: Wesleyan University Press, 1995.

Hanna, Thomas. *The Body of Life: Creating New Pathways for Sensory Awareness and Fluid Movement.* New York: Knopf, 1980.

Hannaford, Carla. *Smart Moves: Why Learning Is Not All in Your Head.* Arlington, Va.: Great Ocean Publishers, 1995.

Hartley, Linda. *The Wisdom of the Body Moving: An Introduction to Body-Mind-Centering.* Berkeley, Calif.: North Atlantic Books, 1995.

Hutchinson, Marcia Germaine. *Transforming Body Image.* Freedom, Calif.: Crossing Press, 1985.

Johnson, Don H. *Bone, Breath, & Gesture: Practices of Embodiment.* Berkeley, Calif.: North Atlantic Books, 1995.

———. *Groundworks: Narratives of Embodiment.* Berkeley, Calif.: North Atlantic Books, 1997.

Johnson, Mark. *The Body in the Mind.* Chicago: University of Chicago Press, 1987.

Jones, Frank Pierce. *Body Awareness in Action: A Study of the Alexander Technique.* New York: Schocken Books, 1979.

Juhan, Dean. *Job's Body: A Handbook for Bodywork.* New York: Station Hill Press, 1987.

Kestenberg, Judith. *The Role of Movement Patterns in Development 1.* New York: Dance Notation Bureau Press, 1977.

Kestenberg, Judith, and Mark Sossin. *The Role of Movement Patterns in Development 2.* New York: Dance Notation Bureau Press, 1979.

Knaster, Mirka. *Discovering the Body's Wisdom.* New York: Bantam Books, 1996.

Kurtz, Ron, and Hector Prestera. *The Body Reveals: An Illustrated Guide to the Psychology of the Body.* New York: Harper & Row/Quicksilver Books, 1976.

Leibowitz, Judith, and Bill Connington. *The Alexander Technique.* New York: Harper & Row, 1990.

Lewis, Penny, and Susan Loman, eds. *The Kestenberg Movement Profile: Its Past, Present Applications and Future Directions.* Keene, N.H.: Antioch New England Graduate School, 1990.

Loman, Susan. *The Body-Mind Connection in Human Movement Analysis.* Keene, N.H.: Antioch New England Graduate School, 1992.

MacDonald, Glynn. *The Complete Illustrated Guide to the Alexander Technique: A Practical Program for Health, Poise, and Fitness.* Thorsons Pub., 1998

———. *Alexander Technique.* London: Headway, 1994.

McCarthy, Kathie. *Wisdom in the Body: Engaging the Body Within a Psychotherapeutic Context,* 1995.

Mechner, Vicki, Editor. *Healing Journeys: The Power of Rubenfeld Synergy.* Chappaqua, New York: OmniQuest Press, 1998.

Olsen, Andrea. *Body Stories: A Guide to Experimental Anatomy.* Barrytown, N.Y.: Station Hill Press, 1991.

Oschman, James, and Nora Oschman. *Energy Medicine: The Scientific Basis.* Edinburgh, New York: Churchill Livingston, 2000.

Park, Glen. *Art of Changing: A New Approach to the Alexander Technique: Moving Toward a More Balanced Expression of the Whole Self.* Freedom, Calif.: Crossing Press, 1998.

Pearsall, Paul. *The Heart's Code: New Findings about Cellular Memories and Their Role in the Mind/Body/Spirit Connection.* New York: Broadway Books, 1998.

Pelletier, Kenneth. *Mind as Healer, Mind as Slayer: A Holistic Approach to Preventing Stress Disorders.* New York: Delta/Seymour Lawrence, 1992.

Pert, Candace. *Molecules of Emotion: Why You Feel the Way You Feel.* New York: Scribner, 1997.

Pierce, Alexandra, and Pierce, Roger. *Expressive Movement: Posture and Action in Daily Life, Sports, and the Performing Arts.* New York, London: Plenium Press, 1989.

Rywerant, Yochanan. *The Feldenkrais Method: Teaching and Handling.* San Francisco: Harper & Row, Publishers, 1983.

Saltonstall, Ellen. *Kinetic Awareness: Discovering Your BodyMind.* New York: Kinetic Awareness Center, 1988.

Shafarman, Stephen. *Awareness Heals: Practical Feldenkrais for Dynamic Health.* London: Thorsons, 1998.

Sweigard, Lulu E. *Human Movement Potential: Its Ideokinetic Facilitation.* New York: Harper & Row, 1974.

Todd, Mabel Ellsworth. *The Thinking Body.* Brooklyn, New York: Dance Horizons, 1968.

Wilentz, Joan Steen. *The Senses of Man.* New York: Thomas Y. Crowell Company, 1968.

Nonprint resources

Hackney, Peggy, Irmgard Bartenieff, and Diane Ramsey. *Discovering Your Expressive Body Concepts in Dance Training Utilizing Bartenieff Fundamentals.* Pennington, N.J.: Dance Horizons Video, 1989. Videocassette.

DANCE PRESERVATION

The sources in this section represent published material related to the preservation of the dance including information about dance libraries, archives, and museums, as well as general information on dance documentation. Dance preservation is a relatively new development, and much of the publications available are in the form of gray literature and electronic publications. The Dance Heritage Coalition meta web site is an excellent source for current information in this area. See also the sections on Dance Notation, Dance and Related Arts, and Dance Ethnology and the Anthropology of Dance.

Print resources

Dance Heritage Coalition. *Sustaining America's Dance Legacy: How the Field of Dance Heritage Can Build Capacity and Broaden Awareness to Dance in the Next Ten Years.* Developed by the National Dance Heritage Leadership Forum, DHC. Washington, D.C.: Dance Heritage Coalition, 2000. URL: www.danceheritage.org

———. *Beyond Memory.* Washington, D.C.: Dance Heritage Coalition, 1994.

Estate Project for Artists with Aids. *A Life in Dance.* New York: Alliance for the Arts, 1999.

For the Record: Documenting Performing Arts Audience Development Initiatives. Washington, D.C.: Arts Presenters Publications, 1999.

Frames of Reference: A Resource Guide from the National Initiative to Preserve America's Dance. Washington, D.C.: Dance/USA, 2001.

Johnson, Catherine J., and Allegra Fuller Snyder. *Securing Our Dance Heritage: Issues In the Documentation and Preservation of Dance.* Washington, D.C.: Council On Library and Information Resources, July 1999.

Keens, William, Leslie Hansen Kopp, and Mindy N. Levine. *Images of American Dance: Documenting and Preserving a Cultural Heritage.* Report on a Study Sponsored by the National Endowment for the Arts and the Andrew W. Mellon Foundation. New York: Preserve, Inc., undated.

Kopp, Leslie Hansen. *Dance Archives: A Practical Manual for Documenting and Preserving the Ephemeral Art*. New York: Preserve, Inc., 1995.

Preserve, Inc. *A Decade of Dance Preservation Symposium*. Conference Proceedings. New York: Preserve, Inc., 1998.

Nonprint resources

National Initiative to Preserve America's Dance. Andrea Snyder, prod. Washington, D.C.: NIPAD, 2001. Videocassette.

Periodical Literature Titles and Addresses of Periodicals' Publishers
This listing includes titles of periodicals dedicated to dance and
dance rsearch, as well as titles of periodicals related to the performing
arts and other related areas, which also include research on dance.
Also included are newspapers that specifically review dance performance and feature dance related articles.

Afterimages. (ISSN 1073-2101) Preserve, Inc., P.O. Box 28, Old
Chelsea Station, New York, NY 10011-0028. E-mail: afterimages@
preserve-inc.org. URL: http://www.preserve-inc.org/pubs.html
American Journal of Dance Therapy. (ISSN 0146-3721) (American
Dance Therapy Association) Subscriptions: c/o Kluwer Academic/
Plenum Publishers, 233 Spring Street, New York, NY 10013-1578.
Also available electronically via Kluwer Online. E-mail: info@
plenum.com. URL: http://www.wkap.nl/journalhome.htm/0146-3721
American Morris Newsletter. c/o Jocelyn Reynolds & Peter
ffoulkes, 2586 36th Avenue, San Francisco, CA 94116. E-mail:
AMN@periodpieces.com. Information at URL: http://web.syr.edu/
%7Ehytelnet/amn/
Attitude: The Dancers' Magazine. (ISSN 0882-3472) Dance Giant
Steps, Inc., 1040 Park Place, Suite C-5, Brooklyn, NY, 11213-1946.
E-mail: dancegiantsteps@hotmail.com; URL: http://idt.net/~beart/
attitude/subscribe.html.
Ballet Review. (ISSN 0522-0653) Editorial: 46 Morton Street, New York,
NY 10014. Subscriptions: 37 W. 12 St., Apt. 7J, New York, NY 10011.
Ballett International/Tanz Aktuell [English ed.] (ISSN 0947-0484)
Editorial: Reinhardtstrasse 29, D-10117, Berlin, Germany. Sub-
scriptions: Friedrich Verlags Service, Postfach 100150, D-30917,
Seelze, Germany. URL: http://www.ballet-tanz.de. U.S. subscrip-
tions: subscribe@glpnews.com; URL: http://www.glpnews.com/TP/
BalletTanz.html.
Ballett-Journal/Das Tanzarchiv. (ISSN 0720-3896) Ulrich Steiner
Verlag, Obersteinbach 5a, D-51429 Bergisch Gladbach, Germany.
E-mail: usteiner@tanzmedien.de.; URL: http://www.tanzmedien.de
Ballroom Dancing Times. (ISSN 0005-4380) Clerkenwell House,
45-47 Clerkenwell Green, London EC1R 0EB, England. E-mail:
ballroom@dancing-times.co.uk.

Brolga: An Australian Journal about Dance. (ISSN 1322-7645) Subscriptions: Ausdance National Secretariat, PO Box 45, Braddon, ACT 2612, Australia. URL: http://ausdance.anu.edu.au/publication/ brolga.html

Cairon. (ISSN 1135-9137) Aula de Danza, Universidad de Alcalá de Henares, Plaza de San Diego, s/n, E-28801 Alcalá de Henares, Madrid, Spain.

Chorégraphie: studie ricerche sulla danza. (ISSN 1125-6230) Editorial: Via Flaminia 158, 00196 Roma, Italy. E-mail: pappacena@uniroma1.it. Subscriptions: Di Giacomo edit., Via Oglio 5, 00198 Roma, Italy.

Choreography and Dance. (ISSN 0891-6381) Subscriptions: P.O. Box 32160, Newark, NJ 07102. E-mail: info@gbhap.com. URL: http://www.gbhap.com.

Columbia-VLA Journal of Law and the Arts. (ISSN 0888-4226) Columbia University School of Law, 435 West 116th St., New York, NY 10027

Congress on Research in Dance. Conference Proceedings (31st, 1998). Congress on Research in Dance, c/o Dept. of Dance, State University of New York, College at Brockport, Brockport, NY 14420-2939.

Contact Quarterly. (ISSN 0198-9634) P.O. Box 603, Northhampton, MA 01061.

CORD Newsletter. (ISSN 0734-4856) Congress on Research in Dance, Dept. of Dance, State University of New York, College at Brockport, 350 New Campus Drive, Brockport, NY 14420-2939. E-mail: ktucker@acspr1.acs.brockport.edu.

Current Biography Yearbook. (ISSN 0084-9499) The H.W. Wilson Company, 950 University Ave., Bronx, NY 10452-4297 URL: http://www.hwwilson.com.

Dance Australia. (ISSN 0159-6330) All correspondence: Dance Australia, GPO Box 606, Sydney, NSW 1041, Australia. E-mail: yaffabiz@flex.com.au.

Dance Chronicle. (ISSN 0147-2526) Editorial: Box 331, Village Station, New York, NY 10014. Subscriptions: Marcel Dekker, Inc., 270 Madison Ave., New York, NY 10016.

Dance Europe. P.O. Box 12661, London E5 9TZ, England.URL: http://www.danceeurope.net.

Dance Gazette. (ISSN 0306-0128) Royal Academy of Dancing, 36 Battersea Square, London SW11 3RA, U.K. E-mail: gazette@

rad.org.uk. URL: http://www.rad.org.uk. U.S. memberships: 15 Franklin Place, Rutherford, NJ 07070. E-mail: rad_usa@hotmail.com.

Dance International. (ISSN 1189-9816) #302-601 Cambie Street, Vancouver, B.C. V6B 2P1 Canada.

Dance Magazine. (ISSN 0011-6009) 111 Myrtle At., #203, Oakland, CA 94607 and 33 W. 60th Street, 10th Floor, New York, NY 10023. Subscriptions: Dance Magazine, P.O. Box 5068 Brentwood, TN 37024-9725. E-mail: dancemag@dancemagazine.com. URL: http://www.dancemagazine.com.

Dance Now. (ISSN 0966-6346) Dance Books, Ltd., 15 Cecil Court, London WC2N 4EZ, England. E-mail: dancebooks@mail.com. URL: http://www.dancebooks.co.uk.

Dance Research. (ISSN 0264-2875) (Society for Dance Research) Orders and sample copies: Edinburgh University Press, Journals Subscriptions Dept., 22 George Square, Edinburgh EH8 9LF, Scotland. Editorial: Richard Ralph, Westminster College, Oxford OX2 9AT, U.K. Society memberships: Peter Bassett, Laban Centre, Laurie Grove, London SE14 6NH, U.K. E-mail: p.bassett@laban.co.uk.

Dance Research Journal. (ISSN 0149-7677) Congress on Research in Dance (CORD), c/o Dept. of Dance, State University of New York, College at Brockport, Brockport, NY 14420-2939. URL: http://www.cordance.org.

Dance Teacher (formerly ***Dance Teacher Now***). (ISSN 0199-1795) Editorial: Lifestyle Ventures, 250 W. 57th St., Suite 420, New York, NY 10017. Subscriptions: Dance Teacher, P.O. Box 1910, Marion, OH 43306-2010. URL: http://www.dance-teacher.com.

Dance Theatre Journal. (ISSN 0264-9160) Laban Centre London, Laurie Grove, London SE14 6NH, U.K. Subscriptions in U.K.: Freepost, Dance Theatre Journal, London, SE 14 6BR, England. E-mail: dtj@laban.co.uk URL: http://195.92.149.143/journal/subscriptions.php3.

DanceView. P. O. Box 34435, Martin Luther King Station, Washington, D.C. 20043.

Dance/USA Journal. (ISSN 1064-6515) Dance/USA, 1156 15th Street NW, Suite 820, Washington, DC 20005-1704. E-mail: danceusa@danceusa.org. URL: http://www.danceusa.org.

Dancing Times. (ISSN 0011-605X) The Dancing Times Limited, Clerkenwell House, 45-47 Clerkenwell Green, London EC1R 0EB, England. E-mail: DT@dancing-times.co.uk; URL: http://www.dt-ltd.dircon.co.uk.

Dancing USA. (ISSN 1053-5454) 200 N. York Road, Elmhurst, IL 60126 URL: http://www.dancingusa.com.

Danser. (ISSN 0755-7639) Editorial: 8, rue de la Terrasse, Paris 17e, France. Subscriptions: BP 68, 77932 Perthes cedex, France.

Danza Italiana. Editorial: c/o Patrizia Veroli, 15 Via Antonio de Berti, 00143 Rome, Italy. Subscriptions: Bulzoni Editore, Via dei Liburni 14, 00185 Rome, Italy.

DCA News. c/o Dance Critics Association, PO Box 1882, Old Chelsea Station, New York, NY 10011.

Drama Review (see *TDR*).

Early Music. (ISSN 0306-1078) Editorial: 70 Baker Street, London W1M 1DJ, U.K.; E-mail: jnl.early-music@oup.co.uk. Subscriptions: Journal Marketing Dept., Oxford University Press, Great Clarendon Street, Oxford OX 2 6DP, England.

Early Music America (ISSN 1083-3633) 11421 ½ Bellflower Rd., Ceveland, OH 44106-3990 URL: http://www.earlymusic.org/Content/EMAg/EMAg.asp.

English Dance and Song. (ISSN 0013-8231) (English Folk Dance and Song Society) Cecil Sharp House, 2 Regent's Park Road, London NW1 7AY, England. URL: http://www.efdss.org.

Ethnomusicology. (ISSN 0014-1836) Society for Ethnomusicology, Morrison Hall, Rm. 005, Indiana University, Bloomington, IN 47405-2501. Subscriptions: University of Illinois Press, 1325 S. Oak Street, Champaign IL 61820-6903; URL: http://www.press.uillinois.edu/journals/ethno.html.

Flamenco! The Journal of Flamenco Artistry. 943 Fifth St., Suite 6, Santa Monica, CA 90403.

Folk Dance Scene. (ISSN 0430-8751) Subscriptions: 2010 Parnell Ave., Los Angeles, CA 90025

Folk Music Journal. (ISSN 0531-9684) English Folk Dance and Song Society, Cecil Sharp House, 2 Regents Park Rd., London NW1 7AY, U.K. URL: http://www.efdss.org.

Habibi. P.O. Box 90936, Santa Barbara, CA 93190-0936. E-mail: Habibipub@aol.com

Hudson Review. (ISSN 0018-702X) 684 Park Ave., New York, NY 10021. E-mail: hudsonreview@erols.com.

Israel Dance. (ISSN 0334-2301) Zoom Hafakot Publishers, 39 Shoham St., Haifa 34679, Israel.

JOPERD : Journal of Physical Education, Recreation and Dance. (ISSN 0730-3084) American Alliance for Health, Physical Education, Recreation and Dance, 1900 Association Drive, Reston, VA 20191. E-mail: joperd@aahperd.org. URL: http://www.aahperd.org.

Journal of Aesthetics and Art Criticism. (ISSN 0021-8529) (American Society for Aesthetics) 404 Cudahy Hall, Marquette University, Milwaukee WI 53201-1881. Subscriptions, e-mail: asastcar@vms.csd.mu.edu. URL: http://www.aesthetics-online.org/asa/asa-info.html, *also* http://www.temple.edu/jaac/

Journal of Dance Medicine & Science. (ISSN 1089-313X) (International Association for Dance Medicine & Science) J. Michael Ryan Publishing, Inc., 24 Crescent Drive North, Andover, NJ 07821-4000.

Medical Problems of Performing Artists. (ISSN 0885-1158) Hanley & Belfus, Inc., 210 S. 13th Street, Philadelphia, PA 19107. URL: http://www.hanleyandbelfus.com/journals/mppa.html

Memoria. (Archives suisses de la danse) Boîte postale 149, CH-1000 Lausanne 13, Switzerland.

Movement Research Performance Journal. (ISSN 1077-0933) Movement Research, Inc., 296 Elizabeth St., #BF, New York, NY 10012. E-mail: movement@pipeline.com

Musical Opinion. (ISSN 0027-4623) 2 Princes Rd., St. Leonards-on-Sea, East Sussex TN37 6EL, England. E-mail: musical-opinion@cwcom.net

New Criterion. (ISSN 0734-0222) Foundation for Cultural Review, 850 Seventh Ave., New York, NY 10019

New Republic. (ISSN 0028-6583) 1220 19th Street NW, Suite 600 Washington, DC 20036. Subscriptions: Box 602, Mt.Morris, IL 61504

New Statesman. (ISSN 1364-7431) New Statesman Ltd., 7th Floor, Victoria Station House, 191 Victoria St., London SW1E 5NE, England. E-mail: sbrasher@newstatesman.co.uk. URL: http://www.newstatesman.co.uk

New Theatre Quarterly. (ISSN 0266-464X) Cambridge University Press, Edinburgh Bldg., Shaftesbury Rd., Cambridge CB2 2RU,

England. E-mail: information@cup.cam.ac.uk. URL: http:// www.cup.cam.ac.uk. North American address: Cambridge University Press, Journals Dept., 40 W. 20th St., New York, NY 10011.

New York Magazine. (ISSN 0028-7369) PRIMEDIA, New York Magazine, 444 Madison Avenue, New York, NY 10022. Subscriptions: New York Magazine, Box 54661, Boulder, CO 80322-4661. URL: http://www.nymag.com

New York Review of Books. (ISSN 0028-7504) 1755 Broadway, 5th. Floor, New York, NY 10019-3780. Subscriptions: Box 420384, Palm Coast, FL 32142-0384. E-mail: mail@nybooks.com. URL: http:// www.nybooks.com/nyrev.

New York Times Book Review. (ISSN 0028-7806) New York Times Company, 229 W. 43rd Street, New York, NY 10036. Subscriptions: Box 9564, Uniondale, NY 11555. URL: http://www.nytimes.com/ books/home/.

New Yorker. (ISSN 0028-792X) New Yorker Magazine, Inc., 20 W. 43rd St., New York, NY 10036-7440. Subscriptions: Box 56447, Boulder, CO 80322. URL: http://www.newyorker.com

Newsweek. (ISSN 0028-9604) 251 W. 57th St., New York, NY 10019-1894. Subscriptions: Box 403, Livingston, NJ 07039. URL: http://www.newsweek-int.com

Opera House: the Magazine of the Royal Ballet, the Royal Opera, and the Birmingham Royal Ballet. (ISSN 1351-3443) Premiere Magazines Ltd., Haymarket House, 1 Oxendon Street, London SW1Y 4EE, England.

Orchestra. (ISSN 0345-7922) Cirila I Metodija 2a/III, Beograd, Yugoslavia. E-mail: orchestrayu@yahoo.com

Performing Arts Resources. (ISSN 0360-3814) Theatre Library Association, Shubert Archive, 149 West 45th St., New York, New York 10036. URL: http://www.brown.edu/Facilities/ University_Library/beyond/TLA/TLA.html

Popular Music. (ISSN 0261-1430) Cambridge University Press, Edinburgh Bldg., Shaftesbury Rd., Cambridge CB2 2RU, England. E-mail: information@cup.cam.ac.uk.
URL: http://www.cup.cam.ac.uk. North American address: Cambridge University Press, Journals Dept., 40 W. 20th St., New York, NY 10011.

Saisons de la Danse. (ISSN 1151-177X) Subscriptions: Dans'press Service Abonnements, 18, av. Daumesnil, 75012, Paris, France.

E-mail: redaction.saisons@wanadoo.fr. URL: http://
www.ladanse.com/les-saisons
Skating. (ISSN 0037-6132) Subscriptions: 20 First Street, Colorado
Springs, CO 80906-3697. Published by the United States Figure
Skating Association, URL: http://www.usfa.org
**Society of Dance History Scholars. Conference Proceedings (21st,
1998).** Marge Maddux, Treasurer, SDHS, Dance Program, Univer-
sity of Minnesota, Barbara Barker Center for Dance, 500 21st
Avenue South, Minneapolis, MN 55455. URL: http://
www.sdhs.org/proceedform.html
Strategies. (ISSN 0892-4562) American Alliance for Health,
Physical Education, and Recreation, 1900 Association Drive, Reston,
VA 20191-1599. E-mail: strategies@aahperd.org. URL: http://
www.aahperd.org.
T D R (The Drama Review) (ISSN 1054 2043) MIT Press, 5
Cambridge Center, Cambridge, MA 02142. E-mail: journals-
orders@mit.edu. URL: http://mitpress.mit.edu. For electronic access
via Project Muse, see http://muse.jhu.edu.
(T D & T)Theatre Design & Technology. (ISSN 1052-6765)
United States Institute for Theatre Technology, 6443 Ridings Road,
Syracuse, NY 13206-1111.
Tanz Affiche. (ISSN 1026-3063) Subscriptions: Eggerthgasse 10/7,
A-1060 Vienna, Austria. E-mail: abo@tanz.at. URL: http://
www.tanz.at.
Tanz und Gymnastik. (Schweizerischer Berufsverband für Tanz und
Gymnastik) Subscriptions: Sekretariat, SBTG, Postfach CH-8032,
Zürich, Switzerland. URL: http://www.tanznetz.ch/vsbt.
Tanzdrama Magazin. (ISSN 0932-8688) (Mary-Wigman
Gesellschaft) Im Media Park 7, 60570, Köln, Germany. Subscrip-
tions: K. Keiser Verlag, Dr. Klaus Kieser, Kreittmayrstrasse 32, 80335
München, Germany.
Tanzen. (ISSN 0724-1062) VTB Verlag Zeitschrift "tanzen",
Uhlandstrasse 1, 72535 Heroldstatt, Germany. E-mail: info@tanzen-
vtb.de. URL: http://www.tanzen-vtb.de.
Theatre Journal. (ISSN 0192-2882) (Association for Theatre in
Higher Education) Johns Hopkins University Press, Journals
Publishing Division, 2715 N. Charles Street, Baltimore, MD
21218. E-mail: jlorder@jhunix.hcf.jhu.edu. URL: http://
muse.jhu.edu.

TLS (Times Literary Supplement). (ISSN 0307-661X) Admiral House, 66-68 East Smithfield, London, E1 9XY, U.K. URL: http://www.the-tls.co.uk.

Vanity Fair. (ISSN 0733-8899) Vogue House, Hanover Sq., London W1R 0AD England. URL: http://www.vanityfair.co.uk.

Viltis. (Ceased publication) (ISSN 0042-6353) International Institute of Wisconsin, 1110 N. Old World Third Street, Suite 420, Milwaukee, WI 53203-1102. Also available in microform from University Microfilms International, 300 North Zeeb Rd., Ann Arbor, MI 48106.

Women and Performance. (ISSN 0740-770X) 721 Broadway, 6th Floor, New York, NY 10003. E-mail: women@echonyc.com. URL: http://www.echonyc.com/~women.

Writings on Dance. (ISSN 0817-3170) P.O. Box 106, Malverne, Victoria 3144, Australia.

Yearbook for Traditional Music. (ISSN 0740-1558) International Council for Traditional Music, c/o Department of Music, MC 1815, Columbia University, 2960 Broadway, New York, NY 10027. E-mail: ictm@compuserve.com. URL: http://www.music.columbia.edu/~ictm.

Current Periodicals Indexed by the NYPL

Afterimages. New York: Preserve, Inc.
ADTA Newsletter
American Dance Therapy Annual Conference Proceedings
American Journal of Dance Therapy
Arts Management
Arts Search
Ballroom Dancing Times
Ballroom review
Contact Quarterly
Country Dance and Song
Dance Chronicle
Dance Research
Dance Research Journal
Dancing U.S.A.
Early Music
Ethnomusicology
Habibi: A Journal for Lovers of Middle Eastern Dance and Arts

Impulse: The International Journal of Dance Science, Medicine, and Education
Journal for the Anthropological Study of Human Movement
Journal of Appalachian Studies Association
Journal of Dance Education
Journal of Dance Medicine & Science
Journal of Health, Physical Education, Recreation and Dance
Journal of the Folklore Institute
Kinesiology and Medicine for Dance
Medical Problems of Performing Artists
Somatics: Magazine-Journal of the Mind/Body Arts and Sciences
Stern's Directory
Visual Anthropology
Women and Performance
Yearbook for traditional music

Discontinued Periodicals to Maintain
Action! Recording! (newsletter published by Laban Centre, London)
Arabesque
Choreologist (published by the Benesh Institute, London)
Dance and Dancers
Dance Index
Dance Notation Journal (published by the Dance Notation Bureau)
The Dance Notation Record (published by the Dance Notation Bureau)
Dance Perspectives
Dance Scope
Israel Dance
Labanotator (published by Labanotation Institute, Surrey)
Viltis

Internet Resources

Metasites:
Dance Heritage Coalition
www.danceheritage.org

Selected Dance Resources on the Internet, New York Public Library
for the Performing Arts, Dance Collection
www.nypl.org/research/lpa/dan/Intro.html

Artslynx International Dance Resources
www.artslynx.org/dance/

Other sites:
ArtsWire, a program of New York Foundation for the Arts
http://www.artswire.org

Preserve, Inc.
www.preserve-inc.org

The Estate Project for Artists with AIDS
www.artistswithaids.org

Folk Dance Association
http://www.folkdancing.org

International Council on Traditional Music
http://music.columbia.edu/~ictm/

Study Group on Ethnochoreology
http://ictm.alteravista.com/index.php3

Cross Cultural Dance Resources
http://www.ccdr.org

English Folk Dance & Song Society
http://www.efdss.org/

Foundation for Pacific Dance
http://home.att.net/~pacificdance/home.html

Jazz dance
Bob Boross Jazz Dance Homepage
http://www.jazzart.org/jdh/history/into.html

Middle Eastern dance:
Morocco. 1997. *Morocco's Meanderings* [on-line]. New York: Morocco and the Casbah Dance Experience; available from http://www.tiac.net/users/morocco

Shira, a.k.a. Julie Elliot. 2000. *The Art of Middle Eastern Dance* [on-line]. Available from http://www.shira.net

Bauer, Eileen. *Mediterranean Dance Mailinglist* [on-line]. To register send an email to majordomo@world.std.com with "subscribe med-dance (without quotes) in the body of the message. Archived at http://www.dancers-archive.com/med-dance

The Morris Ring
http://www.TheMorrisRing.org

National Initiative to Preserve America's Dance (NIPAD)
http://save-as-dance.org/

National Resource Centre for Dance
http://www.surrey.ac.uk/NRCD/nrcd.html

National Museum of the American Indian (Smithsonian Institution)
http://www.si.edu/nmai/nav.html

Pow Wow Dancing
http://www.powwows.com

Somatic Studies:
http://www.northatlanticbooks.com/somatics.html
http://www.alexandertechnique.com/somatics/

http://www.somatics.de/somatics-03.html
http://www.feldenkrais.com/findPractitioner/index.html

Congress on Research in Dance
http://www.cordance.org

Society of Dance History Scholars
http://www.sdhs.org

APPENDIX

Film and Video Distributors
American Dance Festival Video
2355 University Avenue, Suite P
Madison, WI 53705
Phone:(608) 231-1969
Fax:(608) 231-1954
Website: http://www.adfvideo.com

ARC Videodance
123 W. 18th St., 7th floor
New York, NY 10011
Phone: (212) 206-6492

Arthur Cantor, Inc.
1501 Broadway, Suite 403
New York, NY 10036
(800) 237-3801
Phone: (212) 391-2650
Fax: (212) 391-2677
Website: www.arthurcantor.com/film.htm

Applause Productions, Inc.
85 Fernwood Lane
Roslyn, NY 11576
Phone: (800) 277-5287

Baker & Taylor Video
501 S. Gladolus
Momence, IL 60954
Phone: (800) 775-2300
Website: www.baker-taylor.com

Bergh International Holdings, Inc.
5428 Lyndale Ave., S.
Minneapolis, MN 55419
Phone: (800) 423-9685

Biograph Entertainment
2 Depot Plaza, Suite 202-B
Bedford Hills, NY 10507
Phone: (800) 346-3144
Phone: (914) 242-9838
Fax: (914) 242-9854

Bridge to the Tango
P.O. Box 560127
West Medford, MA 02156
Phone: (888) 382-6467 (U.S. and Canada)
Phone: (617) 666-8518 (from other locations)
Fax: (617) 666-4316
Website: http://www.bridgetothetango.com

Buena Vista Home Video (Walt Disney)
3900 West Alameda
Burbank, CA 91505
Phone: (818) 567-5000
Fax: (818) 567-6464

Bullfrong Films
P.O. Box 149
Oley, PA 19547
Phoen: (800) 543-FROG
Phone: (215) 779-8226
Fax: (610) 370-1978
Website: www.bullfrogfilms.com

Canyon Cinema Films
2325 Third Street, Suite 338
San Francisco, CA 94107
Phone: (415) 626-2255
Website: www.canyoncinema.com

Carousel Films
260 Fifth Avenue, Suite 905
New York, NY 10001
Phone: (800) 683-1660

Phone: (212) 683-1660
Fax: (212) 683-1662

Chandra of Damascus Middle East
Dance Center
6706 North West 18th Avenue
Gainesville, FL 32605
Phone: (352) 332-9080

Choreographics
1187 Shattuck Avenue
Berkeley, CA 94707
Phone: (510) 524-9254

Cinema Guild
1697 Broadway, Ste 506
New York, NY 10019
Phone: (212) 246-5522
Fax: (212) 246-5525
(800) 723-5522
Website: www.cinemaguild.com

Columbia Tristar Home Video
Culver City, CA 91505-4627
Phone: (310) 280-8000
Fax: (310) 972-0937
Website: www.cthv.com

Corinth Video
34 Gansevoort St.
New York, NY 10014
Phone: (212) 463-0305
Fax: (212) 929-0010
(800) 221-4720
Website: www.awa.com/video/cvorder.html

Critics' Choice Video, Inc.
P.O. Box 749
Itasca, IL 60143-0749

(800) 367-7765
Website: www.ccvideo.com

Crosscureent Media/NAATA
346 Ninth Street
San Francisco, CA 94130
Phone: (415) 552-9550
Website: www.naatanet.org/distrib

Cunningham Dance Foundation
55 Bethune Street
New York, NY
Phone: (212) 255-3130
Fax: (212) 633-2453
Website: www.merce.org

Dance Film Archive
University of Rochester
Rochester, NY 14627
Phone: (716) 275-5236
Fax: (716) 271-1616

Dance Films Association, Inc.
48 West 21st Street
New York, NY 10010
Phone: (212) 727-0764
Fax: (212) 675-9657
Website: www.dancefilmsassn.org

Dance Horizons Video
Princeton Book Company Publishers
P.O. Box 831
Hightstown, NJ 08520-0831
(800) 220-7149
Phone: (609) 426-0602
Fax: (609) 426-1344
Website: www.dancehorizons.com/videos.html

Dance on Video
620 East 81st Terrace
Kansas City, MO 64131-2123
Phone: (816) 333-7935

Dancing Video
5637 Rosalind Avenue
El Cerrito, CA 94530
Phone: (510) 658-0377
Fax: (510) 235-8730

Direct Cinema Limited
P.O. Box 10003
Santa Monica, CA 90410-9003
Phone: (310) 636-8200
Fax: (310) 636-8228
(800) 525-0000

Documentary Educational Resources
101 Morse Street
Watertown, MA 02472
(800) 569-6621
Phone: (617) 926-0491
Fax: (617) 926-9519
Website: www.xensei.com/docued

Electronic Arts Intermix
536 Broadway, 9th Floor
New York, NY 10012
Phone: (212) 966-4605
Fax: (212) 941-6118
Website: www.eai.org

Facets Multimedia, Inc.
1517 W. Fullerton Ave.
Chicago, IL 60614
Phone: (312) 281-9075
Fax: (312) 929-5437
(800) 331-6197
Website: www.facets.org

Film-makers' Cooperative
175 Lexington Avenue
New York, NY 10016
Phone: (212) 889-3820
Fax: (212) 889-3821
Website: www.film-makerscoop.com/core.htm

Filmakers Library, Inc.
124 E. 40th
New York, NY 10016
Phone: (212) 808-4980
Fax: (212) 808-4983
Website: www.filmakers.com

Films for Humanities And Sciences
P.O. Box 2053
Princeton, NJ 08543-2053
(800) 257-5126
Phone: (609) 275-1400
Fax: (609) 275-3767
Website: www.films.com

First Run/Icarus Films
153 Waverly Pl.
New York, NY 10014
Phone: (212) 727-1711
Fax: (212) 989-7649
(800) 876-1710
Website: www.frif.com

Indiana University
Instructional Support Services
Franklin Hall 0009
Bloomington, IN 47405-5901
(800) 552-8620
Phone: (812) 855-8087
Fax: (812) 855-8404

Ingram International Films
7900 Hickman Rd.
Des Moines, IA 50322
(800) 621-1333
VHS; Beta

Insight Media
2162 Broadway
New York, NY 10024-6642
Phone: (212) 721-6316
Fax: (212) 799-5309
Website: www.insight-media.com

Instructional Video
727 "O" St.
Lincoln, NE 68508-6570
(800) 228-0164
Website: www.insvideo.com

International Film Bureau, Inc.
332 South Michigan Avenue
Chicago, IL 60604-4382
Phone: (312) 427-4545
Fax: (312) 427-4550

Iowa State University
Instructional Technology Center
121 Pearson Hall
Ames, IA 50011-2203
(800) 447-0060
Phone: (515) 294-1540
Fax: (515) 294-8089
Website: www.itc.iastate.edu

Journal Films, Inc.
1560 Sherman Ave., Ste. 100
Evanston, IL 60201
(800) 323-9084

Karol Video
P.O. Box 7600
Wilkes Barre, PA 18773
Phone: (570) 822-8899
Fax: (570) 822-8226
(800) 526-4773

Kinetic Film Enterprises, LTD.
255 Delaware Avenue
Buffalo, NY 14202
(800) 466-7631
Phone: (716) 856-7631
Fax: (716) 856-7838

The Kitchen
512 West 19th Street
New York, New York 10011
Phone: (212) 255-5793
Website: www.thekitchen.org

Kultur Video
195 Hwy. No. 36
West Long Branch, NJ 07764
Phone:(732) 229-2343
Fax: (732) 229-0066
(800) 458-5887
Website: www.kulturvideo.com

Mastervision, Inc.
969 Park Ave.
New York, NY 10028
Phone: (212) 879-0448
Fax: (212) 744-3560
Website: www.masterv.com/indexnofr.htm

Media for the Arts
360 Thames St.
P.O. Box 1011
Newport, Rhode Island 02840
Website: www.art-history.com

Media Guild
11722 Sorrento Valley Rd., Ste. E
San Diego, CA 92121
Phone: (619) 755-9191
Fax: (619) 755-4931
(800) 886-9191
Website: www.mediaguild.com/home.html

Media Home Entertainment
510 W. 6th St., Ste. 1032
Los Angeles, CA 90014
(213) 236-1336

MGM/UA Home Entertainment
2500 Broadway
Santa Monica, CA 90404-3061
(310) 449-3000
Website: www.mgm.com

Michael Blackwood Productions, Inc.
251 W. 57th St.
New York, NY 10019-1802
Phone: (212) 247-4710
Fax: (212) 247-4713
Website: www.panix.com/~blackwoo/

Michigan State University. Instructional Media
Center
East Lansing, MI 48826-0710
(517) 353-9229

Mike LaBell's Video
75 Freemont Pl.
Los Angeles, CA 90005
(213) 938-333

Modern Curriculum Press - MCP
P.O. Box 70935
108 Wilmot Rd.
Chicago, IL 60673-0933
(800) 321-3106

Moonbeam Producations, Inc.
836 Hastings St.
Traverse City, MI 49684
(800) 445-2391

Morocco
320 West 15th Street
New York, NY 10011
Phone: (212) 727-8326
Fax: (212) 463-7116

Movies Unlimited
3015 Daniel Rd.
Philadelphia, PA 19154
Phone: (800) 523-0823
Website: www.moviesunlimited.com

Museum of Modern Art
Circulating Film Library
11 West 53rd Street
New York, NY 10019
Phone: (212) 708-9530
Fax: (212) 708-9531
Website: www.moma.org

Music Video Distributors
N 1410 E. Circle Dr.
Oaks, PA 19456
Phone: (800) 888-0486
Fax: (610) 650-9102
Website: www.musicvideodist.com

Mystic Fire Video, Inc.
P.O. Box 422, Prince Street Station
New York, NY 10012
(800) 292-9001
Phone: (212) 941-0999
Fax: (212) 941-1443
Website: www.mysticfire.com

National Archives
8601 Adelphi Road
College Park, MD 20740
(301) 713-7060
Website: www.nara.gov

National Resource Centre for Dance (NRCD)
University of Surrey
Guildford, Surrey
GU2 5XH
UK
01483-259316
Website: www.surrey.ac.uk/NRCD/memsub.html

New Day Films
22D Holywood Avenue
Ho-Ho-Kus, NJ 07423
Phone: (201) 652-6590
Fax: (201) 652-1973

New Line Home Video
116 North Robertson Boulevard
Los Angeles, CA 90048
Phone: (310) 967-6679
Fax: (310) 854-0602
Website: www.newline.com/shop/huc.html

New Yorker Films
16 West 61st
New York, NY 10023
(800) 447-0196
Phone: (212) 247-6110
Fax: (212) 582-4697
Website: www.newyorkerfilms.com

Orion Enterprises
c/o Jazz Dance World Congress
614 Davis Street
Evanston, IL 60201
Phone: (847) 866-9443/251-4434

New Video Collection
P.O. Box 2284
So. Burlington, VT 05407
Phone: (800) 538-5856
Fax: (802) 864-9846

Paramount Home Video
Bluhdom Bldg.
5555 Melrose Ave.
Los Angeles, CA 90038
(323) 956-8090

PBS Video
P.O. Box 751089
Charlotte, NC 28275
Phone: (703) 739-5000/5383
Fax: (703) 739-0775
(800) 344-3337
Website: www.pbs.org/search

Pennsylvania State University, Audio-Visual Services
Special Services Bldg.
1127 Fox Hill Rd.
University Park, PA 16803-1824

Phone: (814) 865-6314
Fax: (814) 863-2574
(800) 826-0132

Phoenix/BFA Films
2349 Chaffee Dr.
St. Louis, MO 63146
Phone: (314) 569-0211
Fax: (314) 569-2834
(800) 221-1274

Pro Arts International
Nikolais/Louis Dance
611 Broadway, Suite 223
New York, NY 10012
Phone: (212) 420-0700
Fax: (212) 420-0770

Pyramid Film & Video
Box 1048
2801 Colorado Ave.
Santa Monica, CA 90404
Phone: (310) 828-7577
Fax: (310) 453-9083
(800) 421-2304

Sony Music Video Enterprises
550 Madison Ave.
New York, NY 10022
Corporate: (212) 833-7095
Retail: (516) 827-3736
Website: www.sonymusicvideo.com/catalog

Stanford University Documentary
Film and Video Program
3862 23rd Street
San Fransico, CA 94114
(415) 206-9424

Third World Newsreel
545 8th Ave., 10th Floor
New York, NY 10018
Phone: (212) 947-9277
Fax: (212) 594-6417
Website: www.twn.org

UCLA Instructional Media Center
University of California at Los Angeles
46 Powell Library
Los Angeles, CA 90095-1517
Phone: (310) 825-0755
Fax: (310) 206-5392

University of California Extension Ctr. for Media &
Independent Learning
2000 Center St., 4th Floor
Berkeley, CA 94704
Phone: (510) 642-0460
Fax: (510) 643-9271
Website: www-cmil.unex.berkeley.edu/media

University of Minnesota
University Film and Video
1313 Fifth Street SE, Suite 108
Minneapolis, MN 55414
(800) 847-8251
Phone: (612) 627-4270
Fax: (612) 627-4280

University of Washington Educational Media
Collection
Kane Hall, DG-10
Seattle, WA 98195
Phone: (206) 543-9909

Uzbeck Dance and Culture Society
P.O. Box 65195
Washington, DC 20035-5195
Phone: (301) 585-1105

Vestron
c/o Live Home Video
15400 Sherman Way
P.O. Box 10124
Van Nuys, CA 91410-0124
(818) 988-5060

Video Artists International, Inc.
158 Linwood Plaza, Ste.301
Fort Lee, NJ 07024
Phone: (800) 477-7146
Website: www.vaimusic.com

Video Int'l Entertainment World
34 E. 23rd St.
New York, NY 10010
Phone: (212) 674-5550
Fax: (212) 979-0266
(800) 843-9843

Visionary Dance Productions
P.O. Box 30797
Seattle, WA 98103
Phone: (206) 632-2353

Warner Home Video
4000 Warner Blvd.
Burbank, CA 91522
Phone: (818) 954-6000

Warner Reprise Video
3300 Warner Blvd.
Burbank, CA 91505-4694
Phone: (818) 846-9090

Wishing Well Distributing
P.O. Box 1008
Silver Lake, WI 53170
Phone: (800) 888-9355

Women Make Movies
462 Broadway, Ste. 501
New York, NY 10013
Phone: (212) 925-0606
Fax: (212) 925-2052
Website: www.wmm.com

Zipporah Films
1 Richdale Avenue, Unit #4
Cambridge, MA 02140
Phone: (617) 576-3603
Fax: (617) 864-8006
Website: www.zipporah.com/index.html

Out of Print Dance Booksellers
This list offers representative dealers only and is not an endorsement.

Dance Books, Ltd.
dl@dancebooks.co.uk
www.dancebooks.co.uk
street address until Jan. 27, 2000:
9 Cecil Court
London, WC2N 4EZ
England
Telephone: (01) 836-2314
(new address and phone number pending)

The Dance Mart
Box 994
Teaneck, NJ 07666
Telephone: (201) 833-4176

Drama Book Shop
723 7th Avenue at 48th St., 2nd floor
New York, NY 10019
Telephone: (212) 944-0595
Toll free: (800) 322-0595
Fax: (212) 730-8739
http://www.dramabookshop.com/

Stephen Feldman
Asian Rare Books
175 W. 93rd Street, #16-D
New York, NY 10025
Telephone: (212) 316-5334

Friends of Terpsichore
25 Wood St., Suite 1608
Toronto, ON M4Y 2P9
Telephone: (416) 340-9958
Toll Free: (888) 882-9406
Fax: (416) 348-0486
Email: mlos01@ibm.net

Golden Legend
7615 Sunset Blvd.
Los Angeles, CA 90046
Telephone: (323) 850-5520
Fax: (323) 850-1524
e-mail: legenda@ix.netcom.com

J. & J. Lubrano
8 George St.
Great Barrington, MA, 01230
Telephone: (413) 528-5799
Fax: (413) 528-4164
e-mail: lubrano@bcn.net

M M Einhorn Maxwell, Books
80 E. 11 St.
New York, NY 10003
Telephone: (212) 228-6767

Motley Books
P.O. Box 6
Stockbridge
Hants SO20 6HR
Telephone: 01794-388959

Richard Stoddard Performing Arts Books
18 E. 16th Street
New York, NY 10003
Telephone: (212) 645-9576

For Middle Eastern Dance
Artemis
2945 Woodstock Avenue
Silver Spring, MD 20910-1249

Associated Research in Arab Folklore (ARAF)
3270 Kelton Avenue
Los Angeles, CA 90034-3002

Baraka
1700 Church Street, #1265
San Francisco, CA 94131

Morocco
320 West 15th Street
New York, NY 10011

Ramzy Music International
11693 San Vicente Boulevard
PMB 112
Los Angeles, CA 90049

Title Index

Name Index

Aberle, Viola, 58
Abiddin, Zainal Tinggal, 32
Abrahams, Roger D., 38, 40, 79
Acocella, Joan Ross, 20 [Nijinsky], 102 [Levinson], 107 [Levinson]
Adachi, Barbara, 30
Adair, Christy, 104
Adamczyk, Alice J., 37
Adams, Doug, 46
Adamson, Andy, 100
Adrian, Marlene [Cooper], 121
Adshead-Lansdale, Janet, 6, 113
Ahye, Molly, 40
Ailey, Alvin, 9, 67, 71
Ajayi, Omofolabo S., 26
Albright, Ann Cooper, 90
Alcantara, Pedro De, 127
Aldrich, Elizabeth, 2, 56
Alejandro, Reynaldo G., 36
Alexander, Elena, 90
Alexander, F. M., 127, 129 [MacDonald], 130 [Park]
Alexieva, Marguerite [Katsarova-Kukudova], 77
Alhambra Theater [Guest], 56
Ali, Aisha, 36
Allan, Maud, 9
Allcock, Rita, 113
Allemann, Sabine, 61
Allen, Dave [Jordan], 107, 111
Allen, Richard James, 104
Allenby Jaffé, Nigel, 76
Alonso, Alicia, 9
Alter, Judith B., 104
Alvin Ailey American Dance Theater, 63, 67, 71

Amado, Gustavo Rodríguez. See Rodríguez Amado, Gustavo.
Amberg, George, 54
American Ballet School [Dunning], 55
American Ballet Theatre, 54, 57 [Payne], 58, 59, 60, 92
American Dance Festival Company, 68
American Dance Festival, 16
American Indian Dance Theatre, 28
Amoss, Pamela, 46
Anawalt, Sasha, 9, 17, 55
And, Metin, 34
Andersen, Ib, 61
Anderson, Jack, 6, 55, 63, 101, 102 [Martin], 108 [Martin]
Anderson, Laurie, 71
Anderson, Reid, 61
Andersson, Gerd, 58
Andrade, Carlos Alberto G. Coba. See Coba Andrade, Carlos Alberto G.
Andrew W. Mellon Foundation [Keens], 131
Apostolos-Cappadona, Diane [Adams], 46
Appukattan Nair, D. See Nair, D. Appukattan.
Arbeau, Thoinot, 48
Ardolino, Emile, 61, 70
Argentina, La, 19
Arnheim, Daniel D., 121
Arnstam, L., 63
Aroldingen, Karin von, 61
Arpino, Gerald, 9, 59

Subject Index